D0546988

At last! Wisdom from a vetera[...] ministry who survived the perils o[...] soul (and humor) intact, by the grace of a merciful God. Les Stobbe's stories, seasoned with dry wit and unassuming charm, testify to the amazing provision and protection God offers all who are willing to persevere in their calling and invest their sweat, tears, and prayers. The lessons my friend and brother in Christ offers extend beyond the writing world to all who walk by faith and not by sight. I've been privileged to hear these stories from Les himself over nearly thirty years of friendship. They have made all the difference in my writing and spiritual life, adding depth and focus and sparking hope in dark times. I'm so glad to have them to reread and to share with the world. You'll want a copy for yourself and more to give to those you love.

*Lori Stanley Roeleveld, award-winning author of several books including The Art of Hard Conversations and blogger at www.loriroeleveld.com.*

In his ninth decade, my friend and a leading Christian man of letters, takes up his pen yet again to recount "God Moments" in his life as a writer, editor, and publisher, offering compelling counsel to others who would follow on in telling the story.

*John Stockwell, Ph.D., Distinguished Chancellor Emeritus, University of South Carolina Upstate*

I have known Les for over 40 years. He has served me as a friend, proofreader, co-author, editor, publisher, and mentor! Reading his current book has been a joy. Without his assistance I would never have been able to complete my manuscripts or get my work published. Watching his career over the years has motivated me to start my own publishing company and we just published our 104th title under R & R Publishing. This book will be an encouragement to you. You will see a man live a life of faith, struggle and ministry over his lifetime! A verbal testimony is one thing, but a written testimony that allows you to look into his soul as he strives to fulfill God calling, is a much more powerful tool! I will be assigning this book to my counseling clients who struggle with issues of significance!!

*Dr. Jim A. Talley drtalley.com*

Leslie Stobbe has a gift of insight that is astounding. His *Africanus Journal* article on how Luke wrote his gospel, "Earning the Right to Be Published," was selected as a best article of the decade and led off the Tenth Anniversary issue. That Les began his writing life centering on how Jesus communicated is an example of his wisdom. The premier agent in Christian publishing, when I had the blessing to work with him, I met a man of great generosity, with astonishing commitment to help everyone in his vast circle to succeed. The flair and insight of this present book reflect this man. Meeting Les Stobbe in these pages will bless every reader. His is a model life of industry, devotion, and adventure that is not to be missed!

*William David Spencer, Distinguished Adjunct Professor of Theology and the Arts, Gordon-Conwell Theological Seminary, Boston Campus for Urban Ministerial Education, Co-author of* Cave of Little Faces, *Co-founding editor of* Africanus Journal.

It is important to hear the stories of our industry's history. Our confidence in God's divine guidance for the present and for the future is enabled because we can point to His faithfulness in the past. Thank you, Les, for taking us on this fascinating journey.

*Steve Laube, President, The Steve Laube Agency*

Les Stobbe's *God Moments* records some of the best stories from his publishing journey. The stories, like his life, speak of the grace and faithfulness of God. Full of fascinating stories about Christian publishing and showing how God blesses a dedicated life, *God Moments* filled me with hope and joy.

*Sally Apokedak, Apokedak Literary Agency*

I've often marveled at the life experiences of Les. His life story details an incredible life journey punctuated by God Moments. By taking the time to help mold my work and leading me to a path as a successful Christian author, Les Stobbe created a God Moment for me. I thoroughly enjoyed reading about the captivating events that have punctuated his life.

*Andrea Rodgers, Author of At Heaven's Edge: True Stories of Faith and Rescue*

# God Moments
## in My Publishing Life

The Making of a Writer and Publisher

Leslie H. Stobbe

GOD MOMENTS in My Publishing Life
Copyright @ 2021 Leslie H. Stobbe

All rights reserved. No part of this publication may be reproduced or transmitted in any form or by any electronic or mechanical means including photo copying, recording, or any information storage and retrieval system now known or to be invented, without permission in writing from the publisher or the author.

Leslie H. Stobbe
God Moments in My Publishing Life: The Making of a Writer and Publisher
ISBN: 978-1-953114-11-2
Subjects: 1. Religion/General
2. Religion/Christianity/Personal Growth
3. Religion/Christianity/General

Bible Translations Used:
NIV: The New International Version, Zondervan Bible Publishers. Copyright 1978 by New York International Bible Society.
NASB: New American Standard Bible, Copyright: The Lockman Foundation, Copyright 1960, 1962, 1963, 1971, 1973
Publisher: Creation House, Inc. (Used where no version is identified.)
KJB: The Holy Bible Cambridge at the University Press
NKJV: New King James Version, Thomas Nelson Publishers. Copyright 1982, by Thomas Nelson Inc.

Published by EA Books Publishing,
a division of
Living Parables of Central Florida, Inc. a 501c3
EABooksPublishing.com

# TRIBUTES

My first tribute is to God in Jesus Christ and the Holy Spirit, whose God Moments followed me from childhood to the present.

My second tribute is to my wife Rita, who stayed with me and prayed for me, supported me through move after move, often having to take care of the children while I was on trips of all kinds.

A special tribute to Bethany Vander Kaay, our oldest granddaughter, who after college became my assistant, then my webmaster, including posting a chapter every week as I wrote the story of my life as writer and publisher.

The next tribute is to four men already with the Lord, whose trust in me gave me the courage to enter into my God Moments. They are H. F. Klassen, who trusted me to begin a career in publishing after college as founding editor of the Mennonite Observer; Kenneth Taylor, who gave me my start in book publishing; and Robert Walker, who sharpened my writing skills until I could write cover stories in Christian Bookseller Magazine and Christian Life Magazine; and finally Peter Gunther, my protective boss at Moody Press, who supported my God Moment book projects, often against contrary voices in the Editorial Committee. Others will get their recognition in the various chapters.

# CONTENTS

# FOREWORD

I was going to say that my longtime friend, colleague, and mentor, Les Stobbe, is a stellar example of one who finishes well. But he's not finished!

In truth, now in his 90s, Les is still at it. For years I've striven to follow in the footsteps of this giant in Christian writing, editing, and publishing. Maybe it's time I simply surrender to his longevity. From a couple of decades behind, I've watched this physically imposing dynamo becoming the living embodiment of the late Eugene Peterson's idea of "*A long obedience in the same direction.*"

A plainspoken, humble servant type, Les seems to have been everywhere and done everything in an unforgiving profession he felt called to at a young age. In *God Moments*, his straightforward and exhaustive memoir of a man of the Word and a man of words, Les regales us with countless tales from inside Christian publishing's walls.

Even these days, when so many of his colleagues have passed, Les eschews the idea of putting his feet on the desk and gazing out at the greenery. Some years ago he called his local newspaper and offered to deliver one profile per week of players in a nearby music club. He submitted these, each with a photo, and for nine weeks these features captivated readers. Les's name was not even on the pieces, but they generated so much interest that the club oversold an auditorium's capacity for its annual fundraising concert.

And no one was more thrilled than Les, still plying his trade after all these years.

Enjoy his recounting of a life in Christian publishing, where he hobnobbed with everyone from the household names to first time authors. Les was seldom between jobs and always found ways to serve his community, his church, and his God.

I'm proud to call him a friend and highly endorse his memoir. From his vast experience as a journalist, magazine editor, book editor, publishing executive, and literary agent, he showers us with advice from what seems an endless source of wisdom.

Jerry B. Jenkins
The Jerry Jenkins Writers Guild
JerryJenkins.com

# PROLOGUE

I grew up in an era when communicating biblical content remained the primary emphasis in communication. In my first years as a journalist, I was also emphasizing "The Bible says" because that's what I saw modeled and what I was taught. Then I discovered Charles Spurgeon and I found books of sermons reflecting Jesus' style of communication. He employed life illustrations, reflected on how people lived. I started collecting stories to enrich and enhance the appeal of my biblical messages.

In the chapters in which I tell my stories of God Moments I let readers walk in my shoes and experience breakthroughs in life experiences that only God could have orchestrated. In the last five chapters I assume my lifelong role as teacher and mentor of writers. I provide what I learned about what it means to communicate biblically, introducing Jesus as a storyteller and Luke as an amazing historian.

But should today's writers really pay any attention to how Jesus and Luke communicated? If we want to do more than just tell our story or share our insights, I believe the New Testament still provides valid illustrations for communicating for life change. I consider generating attitudinal change and effecting lifestyle change still valid goals for the Christian communicator.

# 1

## God Moments as a Child of the Depression

I was born the year after the 1929 stock market crash. My father had brought my mother from Kansas to Agassiz, British Columbia, Canada, where his parents and brothers and sisters had recently moved after years of trying to make ends meet raising grain crops on rock-filled fields in northern Saskatchewan. I was born in what became a chicken coop once Dad had built a small house.

I was enlisted as a three-year-old to help Dad prepare soil for a vegetable crop when he put me on a horse pulling a plow. I remember falling from it—and being placed right back on it. Dad caught catfish in a creek up the street, which I carried to my mother to prepare for supper—chickens were needed to lay eggs.

In spring I accompanied my dad on his wagon—

adapted from the Model T Ford my father and mother drove from Kansas to British Columbia—selling winter-grown cabbages to neighbors. That wagon served us until I was 14, when Dad could finally afford a well-used Model A Ford. I learned to drive it on our large yard.

My first exposure to foreign mission work came when an uncle arrived from California to report on his family's mission work in South China. I was chasing our cat and got close enough to grab her tail—and was mortified to see I had stripped the fur off her tail just as my uncle drove on the yard. She regrew it.

## Events Shaping My Future

Two other events as a five-year-old reshaped my future—and eventually created opportunities God could use to prepare me for my future vocation. First, scarlet fever invaded our family, causing my eyes to cross. Seven years of social ostracism followed—and I became a book worm to hide from vocal and physical abuse in school. Despite my farm chores and homework, I usually read three church library books a week and two from our school library. Then my mother heard of a chiropractor who had straightened his daughter's eyes. He gladly made the same neck adjustments and performed the same massages on me—and voila! my vision became normal. I never lost my reading habits—great preparation for what God had in mind for me.

Also when I was five the Fraser River rose dramatically from snow melt in the mountains, breaking through the muskrat-weakened dikes along the river near us. I was awakened one night by Dad sloshing through at least a foot of water in my bedroom, picking me up and carrying me to an unfinished second story. There our family of six lived in extremely primitive conditions for two weeks. That convinced my father to follow his family's move into a rented home in Abbotsford, more than 50 files away from Agassiz and on high ground.

Our mother sold inherited property in Henderson, Nebraska, and with the proceeds Dad bought 20 acres that had been logged off ten years earlier. The bonus was that it was a quarter mile from my grandparents and farms by a brother and sister. By the time we bought our property the bushes and trees had grown up to 20 feet among the tree stumps left by loggers, with most of the stumps around six feet in diameter. With me at one end and Dad at the other of a cross-cut saw, we sawed stove-length segments from logs left behind. Using a steel wedge and sledgehammer I could split these large rings small enough to further split the pieces into fuel for Mom's kitchen stove and pot-bellied heater.

The first winter in our rented house the temperature dropped to six below and snow fell several feet deep, though it warmed up quickly enough to melt the snow. Late January I was taken to my grandparent's house nearby. I was brought back in the evening and introduced to a new baby brother, Elmer, born at home.

That spring I was also sent to Saturday German language lessons at our church. I learned to read in what was still our everyday language in our home. Because of my crossed eyes my parents kept me home until I was seven. Yet because I could read German, I quickly picked up English and was reading grade two level English books by Christmas of Grade One. At that point my parents, who had taught school in the U.S., decided to switch to English in our home, preventing younger brothers and sisters from having the embarrassing experiences I had entering first grade not knowing any English.

## Gaining a Financial Foothold

Before he even built a house Dad began clearing an acre, having heard raspberries were a profitable crop. First he blew apart the stumps with stumping powder. As an eight-year-old I carried brush for fires that over a week burned each stump to its roots. Then we dug around the roots, exposing them until we could chop them off below plow level. That fall Dad planted raspberries over two-thirds of a plowed acre. The third year's crop was 10,000 pounds and the income from that crop helped get us out of poverty. Eventually we cleared enough land for two acres of raspberries and two acres of strawberries. The income from those crops supplemented the milk shipments from a growing herd of cows.

Carpenter brothers helped Dad put up a shell of a two-story house—depression circumstances meant interior wallboard was not applied for years. Then he scavenged lumber and tin sheets from a bridge-building project, split cedar roof shingles from blocks sawed from leftover cedar logs—and used tree trunks to frame a barn that could provide shelter for a horse and four cows. I was milking the cows by the time I was 12.

My grandparents and Dad and his brothers and sisters were active in founding and building the initially German-speaking Mennonite Brethren Church. At age six I rode a horse with Dad guiding a scoop that helped dig a basement for a church building less than half a mile from our house. Dad was treasurer for years—Uncle Abe directed the youth choir. In time Uncle John became the pastor while still a farmer with a large family. The rest of the Stobbe family sang in the choir, participated in youth ministry and in other ways. I sang in the Junior Choir, became active as teacher in the Sunday school held in English.

I cannot overlook all the summers we spent in primitive cabins sleeping on straw at hopyards about 20 miles from our house. The picking season typically began in August and might run into mid-September. All five of us missed two weeks of school, but the income generated was also vital to gain stability financially. We had to build a barn equipped to ship milk into the Vancouver market, acquire enough cows to make the dairy financially feasible, acquire electric milking machines, bring in alfalfa hay from B.C.'s interior while we cleared land for pasture. All five of us children graduated from the Mennonite Educational Institute.

## Gaining Independence

The summer I reached 16 I was already six feet tall and nearly 200 pounds of muscle. My parents sent me home each evening of the hop season to milk the cows. At 5:00 p.m. I boarded a two-ton truck equipped with benches on the enclosed back. I was dropped off half a mile from home. After I walked home I rounded up the cows from the pasture, milked them, maybe pumped water, made some supper. Every morning I was up at 4:00 a.m. to find the cows out in the pasture, bring them into the barn, milk them, and send them back to pasture. Then I'd grab a bite and head for the corner to climb aboard the truck for the trip to the hopyard. I picked hops all day, except for a half-hour nap after lunch. That routine lasted for five weeks,

To speed up land-clearing Dad bought two shares in a bulldozer co-op. On reasonably dry days he prepared six stumps for blasting. I'd come home from school and help tamp the stumping powder into a hole slanted under the stump, with a fuse running to the surface from a blasting cap. Each of us would light fuses at three stumps and then run out of range as the explosion split the stump into sizes the bulldozer could push into long rows. Then my job was to keep a fire burning along the stump windrows. It took several months of such effort to prepare three acres for a plow pulled by horses, later a tractor, so we could add to the cow pasture or raise silage corn.

Our mother was a stickler for evening devotions, including reading from the Bible, usually also from

Hurlbutt's Bible Stories for the younger ones, and prayer, were regular until we got into our teens. Then evening chores in the barn and homework filled our time in the evening.

During the time Dad and I worked together land clearing, planted and hoed corn, hoed weeds in the raspberry and strawberry rows, he would share his life experiences and challenges. He illustrated how important hard work, planning ahead, and following Jesus was to being successful in life. There were many God moments that motivated me to be a committed Christ-follower.

Leslie Stobbe

# 2

## Spiritual Development as a Teen

Possibly the best preparation I could have had for entering my teen years were the weekly Bible studies at my grandparents' house. I got to know how God works—and what it means to make Jesus Christ the center of my life—through verse-by-verse studies of the Pauline epistles.

What I did not know at the time was that my grandfather's parents were in the group that left the Mennonite Church in the Ukraine in 1860 to start the Mennonite Brethren Church. It was such an aggressively evangelistic and missionary-oriented new church that members were socially ostracized and several hundred members moved onto a land grant in the foothills of the Caucasian mountains. That heritage came alive in my grandparents, my father and his brothers and sisters—and is now mirrored in our family.

In God's providence an older preacher led a series of prophetic studies at our church, focusing on the Second Coming of Christ. After thinking on it one evening I decided to get ready for that event. The next morning before I headed for school I asked my mother to pray with me. She first introduced me to John 3:16 and then I confessed I was a sinner and accepted the forgiveness Jesus offered. Two years later I asked to be baptized, giving my testimony before the assembled membership of the church. In our Mennonite Brethren Church baptisms commonly happened between ages 15 and 20, so my request was turned down.

**God's Intervention**

In a truly God Moment early the next morning an older couple asked to be baptized at the planned afternoon river baptism. They were asked to give their testimony after the service. A visiting missionary presented the morning message. He related how important his baptism at age nine had been in India. After the service, an elderly visiting preacher got up and suggested my rejection for baptism be reversed—and I was baptized that afternoon. Even at age 12 I recognized the obvious intervention of God in my spiritual development.

A second God Moment happened when my father,

having heard my complaints about the boring teacher in my teen Sunday school class, invited the Sunday school superintendent to our house. I was invited into the room to share my complaint. There was little classroom improvement, but I recognized my father cared about my spiritual development.

My next God Moment came when at age 15 I was promoted to a class of older teen boys. Somehow my complaint about the previous teacher had reached our new teacher. The first quarter our Scripture Press curriculum focused on the book of Jeremiah. Each boy was given a workbook—and our teacher asked me to correct the lessons most of the boys did during the week. What an incredible learning opportunity as I worked my way through 12 to 15 workbooks every Sunday. The fact the boys' work was evaluated every Sunday proved highly motivating for them to actually do the "homework."

## My Parents were Readers

Dad and Mom were readers. My youngest brother remembers Dad reading a book in one hand while doing barn chores. I remember him reading a weekly newspaper. In fact, he even wrote an article for the Free Press Weekly Farmer promoting a family allowance for families with children—later adopted by the Canadian government.

My avid reading habits ran up against our church's library committee's ruling against teens reading fiction before they were 16 years old. So instead, my neighbor friend and I at age 16 were asked to do each Sunday's check-out of library books, an instance of God's sense of humor. I was now free to take home any book I wanted to read. By the fifth grade I was reading eighth grade history texts.

The third year in the senior boys' class the teacher asked me to lead the class when he was on vacation. He also introduced me to a series of apologetic books by Harry Rimmer, then a renowned apologetics writer. That exposure whetted my appetite for biblical apologetics—and prepared me for the apologetic books I acquired as Moody Press editor years later.

## Active in Outreach

Three other teen developments shaped my future. One summer my neighbor and I organized a Sunday afternoon Bible study for teen boys. The preparation alone deepened my knowledge of God's Word. The other was that at age 18 my neighbor and I both taught a class of preteen boys at our church's Sunday school. During the winter he and I also drove to a mission outreach to lead a Sunday school class. We were busy!!

Finally, at age 15 my parents enrolled my sister and me in the ninth grade at the very new Mennonite Educational Institute. For four years we had Bible classes every day based on material prepared by the provincial government's education department. This truly remarkable series of studies of both Old and New Testament events and literary passages, along with regular Scripture verses memorization, prepared me to skip the first two years of our nearby four-year Bible Institute.

## Attending MEI

Of course, we did not only have Bible classes at MEI. I got my first introduction to agricultural practices through, of all persons, our English teacher. I absorbed everything he taught and went home and introduced my father to, for example, crop rotation, the nitrogen delivered by thunderstorms. When he finally was able to have a deep well drilled and strong pump installed, he developed pasture management irrigation practices that won him Master Farmer of the Year Award in our municipality. My efforts to become a softball pitcher in our hayloft, however, only proved I was better at pitching hay bales than softballs.

Another teacher in a health class introduced us to the physical and mental issues that my sister and I recognized were troubling our mother, despite her strong support of our educational objectives. The extraordinary election win of Harry S. Truman in 1948 led me to write an essay on his win for our English class. I had never gained an A in any written assignment by our tough English teacher, but the Truman-win essay got me an A-, a portent of what was to come for me as writer.

By age 19 an uncle had me preaching regularly at a

church planting outreach in a neighboring community. He also provided transportation for me to do mission outreach vacation Bible school.

I still had no idea what God was preparing me for, but I began to get a hint when four of us agreed to work at a silver and zinc mine in northern British Columbia. That story follows in my next chapter.

# 3

## An Inauspicious Start

A question many ask is, "How does God lead us into our life assignment?" God's first hint at an answer for me came on a hospital bed in northern British Columbia, Canada.

Let me set the stage. I had completed my sophomore year at the University of British Columbia when three friends and I motored 800 miles into northern British Columbia for a summer job at a silver, lead, and zinc mine. The location would give us an opportunity to give a lift to the church planting efforts of two uncles and their families. On weekends we worked with young people, delivered sermons and wrote skits, and the four of us sang as a quartet in church and at street meetings in a nearby town populated largely by First Nations residents. On weekdays we went to the mine.

Working with a miner blasting out a vein of ore and shoveling it into chutes, then helping put up four-to-five-foot posts to keep ceilings from coming down, and finally helping fill the ore cars from the chutes, gave me a good introduction to life underground. I particularly enjoyed coming to the surface for lunch at midnight to see the sun rimming the tops of the mountains nearby.

## A Life Commitment

That all changed when the First Aid Man and warehouse manager had a heart attack. I had gained an Industrial First Aid Certificate at evening school the previous summer, so I stepped into his position. After I had handed out drill bits and sold rubber boots at the start of a shift, I had time on my hands, which for a week I devoted to Bible reading and prayer in hopes of discovering God's will for my life. God used Moses' experience and God's challenge to Ezekiel, along with a biography of Charles Spurgeon, to lead me to a commitment to serve the Master on a worldwide basis to the maximum of my capabilities. If Spurgeon could preach every Sunday to 10,000 in London, England, surely he could equip me for an assignment with worldwide reach.

One Saturday I joined male cousins and the men in our quartet on a mountain climbing outing to see if we could reach the top of a nearby 5,000-foot mountain. Fog prevented us from reaching our goal, so we stopped at the edge of a deep ravine created by a rockfall. While the rest climbed to the top of the promontory at the head of the ravine, I decided to rest on the edge of the ravine with my bent left leg against one rock and the other stretched out against another. Looking up I saw a cousin and my best friend roll a large rock to the edge of the promontory. My yells upwind were not heard. When the rock crashed into the ravine, it sent many rocks flying downward, but none came as far as I was. Then I saw them roll an even larger rock to the edge—and again my yelling was not heard. Like projectiles, small rocks rushed by below me, but one took off in my direction. It seemed the rock would miss me, but instead, it hit my left knee a glancing blow and I knew I was in serious trouble.

One friend stayed with me while the rest hurried down to get a stretcher. Using my first aid know-how I had my friend build a splint around my 90-degree knee joint. Twelve hours later we arrived at the small mission hospital, where the doctor straightened my leg and took x-rays, which showed a dislocated knee and split femur. I had no idea I would spend four months in that hospital with a primitive Thomas splint, not once getting off the bed for three and a half months.

## Seizing an Opportunity

But that, too, proved to be God's plan. Some months earlier I had ordered a subscription to Christian Life Magazine. Paging through it one day I saw an ad that screamed at me "You Can Write." The description revealed I could buy seven lessons in The Beginning Christian Writer for $15 from Christian Writers Institute in Chicago. I decided I could afford that, but when the first lesson arrived, I realized I could not do it flat on my back in a four-bed hospital room. Yes, the other three occupants, usually First Nation men, were colorful enough, but I could not get at my typewriter. A mother-daughter nursing team giving me back rubs also entertained me with their story of twice escaping communist revolutions. First the mother's family escaped from Soviet Russia into China after the 1917 Revolution. Then mother and daughter came to Canada to escape the Mao-led revolution in China.

The following April, after rehabbing my leg riding a bicycle on gravel roads, I signed on as despatcher with the B.C. Forest Service and was dropped off at a small fishing island between Vancouver Island and the Mainland. Now I could complete the journalism lessons, writing articles about a new principal at a high school, new ministers at two churches, VBS workers that arrived from Marine Medical Mission.

Delivering the articles to the weekly newspaper editor, I discovered he had taken a journalism course from Newspaper Institute of America. He graciously loaned me his lesson materials. Another God moment. Though I didn't know it when I was writing those first articles in the remote fishing village, God had a plan for me. Ten years later my desk as editor of Christian Bookseller Magazine at Christian Life Publications in Wheaton, IL was next to Janice Franzen, one of the mentors who guided me through the initial lesson assignments.

## The Breakthrough

Completing my summer as B.C. Forest Service dispatcher in the fall of 1953, I headed for the Mennonite Brethren Bible College in Winnipeg, where God took me a giant step forward toward a career in journalism. The president asked me to be the college's publicist because he knew I was already writing feature articles for a Mennonite publication.

The God moment came when, selling our college yearbook in a contest, I landed on the front porch of the publisher at Christian Press. I had done some proofreading and paste-up for him, so I was not surprised when he invited me to sit down. Then he dropped a bombshell. Would I be willing to become editor of a denominational weekly he was hoping to begin in the fall. After a week of prayer, I agreed. At the conference where the Board approved the venture and me as editor, I heard a local soloist with an extraordinary voice. When she showed up at the college that fall, we connected and one year later Rita Langemann became my wife and brought a lot of music into my life.

When I began my first week as editor and realized I would have no assistant or secretary, I initiated 15 minutes of speed typing every day, getting to 85 words per minute. Not only was that a huge assist during the four years I edited a 12-page denominational weekly, it became invaluable as a book author. I wrote weekly editorials, feature articles, and wrote book reviews. I assigned devotionals and a children's feature.

Through the Evangelical Press Association, many of my editorials were reprinted in denominational publications, including The Alliance Witness, edited by A.W. Tozer, already a well-known book author. I also trained church reporters and managed circulation. Seeing only German books in the bookstore I accepted an opportunity as buyer for English language books, not realizing I would soon be managing the selling floor of the Moody Bible Institute bookstore in Chicago when God took my career in a new direction.

My next big God moment came courtesy of Kenneth Taylor, translator of *The Living Bible*. I'll leave that for the next chapter in this series.

# 4

## Becoming Kenneth Taylor's Assistant

To portray how another God moment developed I must begin at Christmas 1954, when I was one of seven students at Mennonite Brethren Bible College in Winnipeg who boarded a bus with Intervarsity students from two universities for Urbana, IL. We joined about 15,000 being challenged to be missionaries. I got two interviews, one with the director of Radio ELWA in Africa and the other with Kenneth N. Taylor, director of Moody Press. I left the interview with him impressed but unaware our paths were to cross six years later in a God Moment.

After completing four years as editor of Mennonite Observer I felt I had learned all I could. I had balanced the store inventory between English and German. I had heard Bill Moore extoll the values in joining the quite new

Christian Booksellers Association. A couple of months later I wrote Moody Press and asked if there might be an opening. With no position available, I joined the faculty of my alma mater, the Mennonite Educational Institute in my hometown, Abbotsford, British Columbia, Canada, not even dreaming that grading 250 essays several times a year was God's preparation for another assignment.

The following February I received a forwarded letter from Human Resources at Moody Bible Institute saying, "In light of openings, please complete the enclosed application." What I didn't know was that Kenneth Taylor had saved my previous year's letter in a file, pulled it out and sent it to HR, asking them to contact me. A God Moment in the making.

## A Publishing Opportunity Surfaces

We were living in my home community near my parents. I had a job as teacher. Why move again? Six weeks later, with the Holy Spirit's prompting I completed the application form but inserted that it would take a supervisory job to get us to Chicago. God kindly disregarded my fleshly proviso and within a week a telegram arrived, "Will send airfare. When can you come?" Our son had just been born, so I telegraphed, "When I get my wife home from the hospital I will come." I engaged a neighbor girl to stay with my wife while I flew to Chicago for the interview.

After a red-eye special I arrived at recently opened

O'Hare Airport at 6:30 a.m. and was whisked to Moody Bible Institute. Four interviews later I left Chicago behind, via Midway Airport—and was home before midnight. While landing at Seattle I gained the assurance I would be offered a position as selling floor supervisor of the Moody Bookstore—and I was. Getting a green card took three months. Getting to Chicago created its own set of problems, with the U-Haul trailer being towed the last 400 miles when my car's engine blew up. Once I found an apartment I had my family come from my wife's parents by train.

I loved my position in the bookstore. I had seven really capable store clerks, plus three students part-time, one of whom set up our Spanish section and later became president of a large Latin American mission. I soon realized that in addition to daytime students Moody had a large number of African Americans as evening school students, most of them so poor they bought books on layaway, paying a dollar a week. We also had men who would steal a Bible or reference book in our downtown store and then try to turn them in for cash at our Institute store. Again and again God had me read into a book at lunch, only to have a customer come in who needed exactly that book.

Another God Moment came when one day Rita commented, "I'd like to participate in one of the Moody radio dramas." When Chuck Christianson, director of Moody radio drama, came into the bookstore I asked if they ever had auditions. Yes, indeed, they would be having an audition in the near future. I asked for an application and took it home. Unconvinced she could handle the role, Rita would not tackle the application, so I did it for her. Most reluctantly, she signed it. A few weeks later she became the lead female character, Hazel, in "Sailor Sam." In subsequent years she played many other roles in radio drama in addition to singing in several radio choirs and serving evening school music students as vocal coach.

## A Brown Envelope Represents the Future

Four months into my job I became acting pastor of a small Evangelical Free Church near our apartment. Six months into my job in another God Moment my boss, Mr. Bixby, brought me a brown envelope and said, "Ken Taylor would like you to evaluate what's in it and report on it at the next editorial committee meeting."

At home I discovered the envelope was a new translation of First Timothy. Having studied Greek, and been a writer/editor, I did a thorough evaluation. At the committee meeting my turn came and I reported, "I've compared this new translation of First Timothy with the Greek and it is really quite accurate. It does need some help with punctuation and active verbs. By the way, whose is it?"

Ken Taylor looked down and murmured, "It is not known" and I knew instantly it was his—and got beet red. My goose was cooked for sure, I thought, since he ran Moody Press. In reality, it was another God moment.

Several weeks later Ken called me up to his office, saying that he would soon be leaving for his vacation. He would provide me with an office, telling me, "I am asking that all incoming manuscripts and proposals be given to you. Evaluate them, rejecting those you think we should not publish and put those we need to consider publishing on my desk." A few weeks later he brought me the manuscript for *The Living Letters*, asking me to edit them. After editing several pages I realized I did not have time to complete that task, what with spending half my time evaluating manuscripts, half my time in charge of a staff of 10 in the bookstore, and evenings preparing sermons for my role as acting pastor.

*Living Letters* never came up for a vote in the editorial committee because Ken took it to Moody Bible Institute President Culbertson's office and introduced what he had done, asking for the president's opinion. Dr. Culbertson expressed reservations about Moody Press releasing another Bible translation. That settled it for Ken, who tried to interest several other publishers, but none would touch it.

## A Manuscript Changes My Prayer Focus

For 18 months I served Kenneth Taylor as manuscript evaluator, stumbling into another God Moment. One of the numerous fine book manuscripts I passed on to the editorial committee was *I Live By Faith,* by Mike Martin, an extraordinary West Coast leader who believed in pinpoint praying. By that time we as family were moving into the main floor of a home several miles from the church. With two toddlers I could not see us navigating two bus transfers in bitter winter weather. With tears dropping I prayed,

"Lord, we need a car, but we don't even have a down-payment. Please provide."

Two weeks later a non-member of the church asked if we needed a car. When I admitted we did, he invited me to his mother's apartment and gave me enough for a down-payment. That experience so bolstered my faith that pinpoint praying became regular with me—and God answered in incredible ways year after year.

All good things must come to an end, and in late summer 1962 Kenneth Taylor was moved from the position of director of Moody Press, while keeping his role as director of Moody Literature Mission—and that started him on the road to becoming his own publisher. Meanwhile I answered an ad for an editor and joined Christian Life Publications as editor of *Christian Bookstore Journal* and associate editor of Christian Life. The God Moments that opportunity provided will be revealed in my next chapter.

# 5

## God's Turn in the Road Enables Skills Development

What can you do when the person who hired and empowered you is moved? Hope for the best? Pray like crazy? Or all of the above?

I engaged in the focused prayer I had learned from Mike Martin's book, *I Live By Faith*. Paging through Intervarsity's *His Magazine* I spied an ad inviting applications for an editorial position—no indication who was looking for an editor. I responded and discovered Christian Life Publications was looking for an editor for *Christian Bookseller Magazine*. Suddenly six years of bookstore experience, matched with four years as weekly denominational publication editor, seemed like a good match.

The fall of 1962 I had a desk in an office on Wacker Drive on the edge of downtown Chicago. My sign said

Editor, *Christian Bookseller Magazine,* but I was also associate editor of *Christian Life Magazine.* I began experiencing one God Moment after another.

Robert Walker, owner and CEO of Christian Life Publications, had a Master's Degree in journalism from Northwestern University, had worked at Moody Press as a young man, and ventured out on his own to bring the Christian reading public the finest level of journalism possible.

When I joined Bob's team he had already been publishing Christian Life Magazine for at least 15 years, had added Christian Bookseller Magazine when the Christian bookstore movement was just gaining momentum, and initiated Christian Camps and Conferences Magazine to give the growing camp and conference movement a voice. He had founded Christian Writers Institute—and it was his ad for the Beginning Christian Writer that God used to turn my life strongly toward journalism ten years earlier.

## Covering the Charismatic Renewal

Bob believed the charismatic movement sweeping the U.S. was of the Holy Spirit and had been reporting on it before I arrived. I came from an anti-charismatic background and Bob and I discussed his approach during the hiring interview. His humility impressed me when at my suggestion he agreed we would not report on charismatic revivals until there was abundant evidence they were of God. Remarkably, he gave me veto power when I sensed strange fire at work. A true God Moment came later when Bob taught me how to engage in spiritual warfare praying.

What I did not realize was that God had thrust me into an intense skills development experience. Bob paid for evening classes on magazine production and on feature writing at Medill School of Journalism in downtown Chicago. He edited every article I wrote over four years. We had regular meetings to analyze secular publications for what we could learn from their journalistic techniques. Every month he brought in a magazine designer and as editorial team we analyzed the presentation of articles in what Bob called the "editorial well" in the center of the magazine. I had no inkling that in a few years I would be doing the layout for two Canadian business magazines.

### God Moments as a Feature Article Writer for *Christian Life Magazine:*

- Writing a cover article on Tom Skinner, an African American Harlem gang leader who turned to Christ when he came upon a Christian radio station and heard a speaker that spoke directly to him. He became the voice of African American Christians as he spoke to white audiences on race relations. During that trip I also interviewed a group of drug addicts who had been won to Christ.
- Writing a cover story on David Wilkerson, author of *The Cross and the Switchblade,* during a Rockford, Ill. crusade and seeing a large group commit their

lives to Christ. Teen Challenge grew out of his ministry.

- Interviewing the 1965 Miss America, Vonda Kay VanDyke, with a tape recorder in the back seat of a car transporting her between book-signings in Christian bookstores—and then spending the evening with her parents. The next morning I took photos of her on the flat roof of their home that not only graced the cover of the magazine but were used for at least a year in circulation promotion.

- Robert Walker and I interviewed Bruce Olson at the O'Hare airport. He was on his way home as the first white man to penetrate the jungle in Bari, then called the Motilone territory on the border between Colombia and Venezuela. Since then it has become a Christian tribe bringing the Gospel to 16 other tribes—and Bruce is still ministering with them. I used my notes to write an article the Chicago Tribune ran in their weekend magazine, six pages with photos I got from Bruce.

Serving as editor of *Christian Bookseller Magazine* provided other learning opportunities. I traveled to New York City to interview editors on new books they were developing. Every month I interviewed Christian bookstore owners on what they were doing to be successful. Bill Moore, executive director of CBA, and I drove to Grand Rapids and visited the first store of a planned Zondervan chain that became Family Bookstores. My wife, Rita, and I manned the information booth at the Christian Booksellers

Convention. I introduced Kenneth Taylor's *Living Letters* to booksellers in the magazine, taking a picture of Ken in his garage holding a pile of his books, which had been a Billy Graham giveaway. Five hundred thousand asked for *Living Letters* and the distribution helped launch the sales of it nationwide.

## God's Provision for a Home

When Bob decided to move his offices to Carol Stream, Ill., next to Wheaton, we faced a crisis as family. I told God about it. "God, we need to rent a house in Wheaton, but there are no rentals. Please provide money for a down payment." A few weeks later a David C. Cook Publishing editor and book author, Joe Bayly, spoke at our Christian Writers Institute writers' conference. Then a God Moment. Joe approached me, asking if I might be interested in editing and revising adult curriculum. They were between editors and badly needed help.

"I can give it a try," I replied. The next day he brought me four student lessons. I worked about five hours a night for each lesson on a 15-year-old portable typewriter—and then two nights for teacher lessons. In six months of editing God provided the down payment on a house vacated by friends who served in radio drama at Moody Radio with Rita. Once in the house with our two children, Carol and Gerald, God also provided an opportunity to write ad copy for a local agency—and newsletters for a Baptist General Conference foreign missions agency. Both not only providing needed extra income as homeowner but also prepared me for a God Moment years later.

In the next chapter I'll reveal why after four years with Robert Walker I followed a friend's invitation to join his business magazine chain in western Canada. A sneak peek—it all started when I used a red pen to mark all grammatical errors, spelling mistakes, awkward sentences, in an issue of my friend's magazine—and sent it to him.

.

# 6

## Responding to a Friend's Challenge

Since I'd committed to serve the Lord on a worldwide basis, why should I accept a challenge by a Canadian friend? Answer: because it was a bodacious challenge. George Derksen and I became acquainted when he was a newspaper reporter in Winnipeg, Canada. What I did not know was that he harbored a dream far bigger than a job at a newspaper. My involvement in that dream started with me daring to criticize a new publishing project of his, a business magazine for his home province, Manitoba. He had already added a Saskatchewan Business Journal when he sent me a copy of the Journal. I decided it needed an evaluation and knew he could handle a critique. So I grabbed a red pen and highlighted spelling, grammatical, and sentence construction errors, as well as descriptions under photos. He laughed so hard he could hardly pick up the phone to call me.

I was busy preparing a message for a German-speaking congregation in Benton Harbor, MI when the phone call came.

"Les, will you come join me as editorial director for my growing chain of business magazines? My goal is to capture Canadian publications for Christ, to be a Christian Lord Thomson, and I need you to join me in that endeavor. May I come and talk with you about it?"

I invited him to join us for the weekend—and the trip to Benton Harbor, MI where the weather alternated between sun and snow showers. But God was there, blessing the morning service and our conversation, becoming another God Moment. Two months later we were on the road with my wife, Rita, a longtime friend of George's wife Dorothy, driving the car, with me at the steering wheel of a U-Haul truck. We arrived in Winnipeg in mid-April, with the Red River in full flood mode, shutting down our usual entry station and usual routes into the city. We drove in on dikes and got to our friend's house.

**Interviews, Interviews, Interviews**

Over four years I got to interview leading businessmen and town and city leaders in most communities in Western Canada. In Manitoba I learned about Junior League hockey in Flin Flon preparing players for the NHL, about Ukrainian culture in Dauphin, about high-rise construction in Winnipeg, fishing, wild rice production, grain growing and processing, about the potato king, and the industries, like a potato chip plant, whitefish shipped to Chicago, inventors of agricultural equipment and automobile accessories. I did stories on innovative advancements in healthcare, the application of new-fangled computers to architectural design. The Lord had me continue my ministry of providing sermons oriented to practical Christian living, plus serving as chair of the Christian Education Committee. Rita quickly became immersed in choral and solo work in the church and the community.

A key God Moment was participating in my second Billy Graham Crusade, the first being the Chicago Crusade in 1962. This time my boss did the fundraising, while I was active in the local Christian Businessmen's Committee promoting the Crusade. God brought many to faith in Christ during that Crusade.

Another God Moment came when as CBMC leadership we brought Tom Skinner, an African American speaker from New York to Winnipeg as speaker for the more than 600 at our Christmas banquet. I helped him spend the previous week visiting prisons, being interviewed on radio and TV. A Christian radio station recorded his banquet address and re-broadcast it three months later— and CFAM told me it had the largest listening audience of any program they had aired.

## Reconnecting with My Heritage

I entered Saskatchewan to read proofs for weeks at the printer—and reconnected with extended family, since my father was 11 when his parents landed there as German-speaking Mennonite immigrants from the Caucasian Mountains. At 23 he traveled to Hillsboro, KS to get his high school education. There he met my mother, born to Mennonite immigrants from the 1870s, who taught school. He drove a Model T over the mountains to Bible Institute of Los Angeles, then north to British Columbia, where his parents had moved and I was born and raised during the depression.

In Saskatoon, SK I ventured onto a golf course for the first time, participated in a celebration of the life of Gordie Howe, one of the Detroit Red Wing greats. With the Derksens and my wife we flew in two four-seater aircraft to a northern lake for a weekend with legendary teen fiction writer Bernard Palmer. We caught Northerns every time we trolled through a bay on the lake. I was unaware that four years later I would become his Bernard Palmer's editor. I visited wheat, oat, barley and canola fields all over the province. Potash mining was just underway, and oil was being extracted—today it's being exploited as an example of fracking success.

In Alberta I surfaced an agricultural editor, Don Sylvester, willing to become editor of the *Alberta Business Journal*--and helped Richard Horch, a Manitoba salesman and musician, settle in as advertising manager. I interviewed business and civic leaders all over Edmonton, Red Deer, Calgary, and Lethbridge. I attended the Calgary Stampede, wrote up the sugar beet industry, dry land grain growing and irrigated crops of all kinds. I wrote a major story on oil being extracted from the tar sands. I covered the arrival of the Colonel and Kentucky Fried Chicken, and cheered for the Calgary Stampeder's football team.

## Back to My Home

Then it was on to my home province, British Columbia, where as family we settled into Langley, from where I could visit my parents in 30 minutes or drive into my office in Vancouver in the opposite direction in about the same time. I had moved from the prairie provinces to "Beautiful British Columbia," with its mountains of timber, coal and mines delivering a variety of mineral ores, logging and lumber, and paper mills—much of it shipped to Japan from the Vancouver ports. I was back where I had worked in a mine, injured my leg mountain climbing, and wrote the articles that became lessons in journalism and prepared me for a life in journalism and book publishing.

I traveled throughout the province doing special issues of the British Columbia Business Journal on the fruit and wine industry in the beautiful Okanagan Valley, to the smelters still spewing noxious substances into the air in Trail. I visited lumber processing mills, walked through smelly pulp and paper mills. I saw a cousin and his family growing tomatoes 600 miles north of the U.S. border near St. John on the Alaska Highway, I wrote a special issue for the dedication of a super port, where unit cars with coal from the Kootenay Mountains unloaded into giant ships bound for Japan. Another issue was devoted to the construction of Vancouver skyscrapers, then one on Victoria, with its gorgeous Butchart Gardens.

## Hitching a Ride to Japan

Meeting Peter Allinger proved to be a God Moment. When I was 12 years old our family visited a small church one Sunday evening. There Peter Allinger, a Christian movie missionary, showed a very new Moody Institute of Science film. While entranced, I did not know that years later he would still be showing Christian films in a theater in Vancouver and running a business serving churches and businessmen with new Japanese 16mm projectors.

I had come to interview Allinger when he revealed he had chartered a plane and was taking top-selling dealers of his projectors on a tour of the factory and other sites in Japan. I quickly suggested that since he had empty seats he could take my wife and me along in return for a full story on his business. I'd also prepare a news release the dealers could use on their return home.

In Japan I did five major interviews, including the chairman of Honda, and wrote up a Japanese corporation starting with iron ore and converting it into everything from medical instruments to large earth-moving equipment. My wife and I attended the world expo in Osaka, where I interviewed the Canadian Government representative—and serendipitously my wife Rita got to visit with the president of Panasonic in the hotel lobby. He had come for the Osaka World Expo and was killing time in the lobby, when he saw this obvious foreigner and decided he wanted to learn a little more English. After introductory exchanges and conversation his daughter arrived and they were off to the Expo.

By the spring of 1970 I had become weary of writing 40 or so articles for every issue of the business magazine. I mentally looked at myself in the mirror and asked, "What would you rather do than anything else in the world?" My answer was, "I'd rather be a Christian book editor." About four months later I responded to a phone call from Moody Press, asking if I'd be interested in interviewing for editor of Moody Press, a position I had hoped to gain eight years earlier.

The next chapter takes me back into a world of books and interaction with writers of all kinds, but also a surprise God Moment with far-reaching implications as a writer.

# 7

## My U-Turn into Books

In 1970 my God Moment, the invitation from Moody Bible Institute to head up the editorial department of Moody Press, became a long-term U-turn in our family's life. As family we settled back into the Glen Ellyn/Wheaton area 30 miles west of downtown Chicago, the community we had left four years earlier. I began life as a commuter, first in a carpool and then by train, which let me read a daily newspaper on the way home and process correspondence with writers on the way to work.

Unfortunately, our house in British Columbia took six months to sell. God knew I was not earning enough to sustain two mortgages, so he implemented another God Moment. I received a call from Bill Krutza, a member of the church we attended.

"Les, the new Urban Ministries curriculum for inner city kids needs a junior high writer. Would this interest you? Henry Soles will be the editor and you will be working with him."

I had taught Sunday school in every church we attended, from preteen to adult, but a white Canadian writing curriculum for mostly African American kids in the inner city? Then I remembered the swarms of neighborhood African American boys who'd regularly flood Moody Bookstore—and the African American men and women filling the store two evenings a week to buy books on their way to Moody Evening School classes. As a writer I had developed at least some cross-cultural sensitivities.

"I'll tackle it if Henry Soles will acculturate what I write," I responded.

For two years I spent many evenings writing lessons for African American junior high kids and turning them over to Henry Soles, a delightful person and former Newark, NJ daily reporter. But God was not finished with my acculturation.

## A Dallas Expo God Moment

In 1972 Moody Press agreed to send me to Campus Crusade for Christ's Expo for college students in Dallas—and another God Moment occurred. I had attended the evening meeting in the 100,000-seat Cotton Bowl, where Billy Graham had challenged the students filling the Cotton Bowl. Arriving at my hotel I headed for the restaurant.

Looking around, I spotted only one empty seat opposite an African American. I sat down, extended my hand and gave my name. He responded with, "I'm John Perkins."

His name rang a bell. I had read about an African American Christian leader in Mississippi who had been badly beaten by a sheriff after he inquired about young men he was mentoring being imprisoned for no reason. I immediately sensed a story, having earlier told the story of another African American leader, Tom Skinner, for *Christian Life Magazine*. In my conversation with John Perkins I discovered he had loaned four of his converts to the Gospel to Campus Crusade in an effort by Bill Bright to enlist African American students for Expo. Later I had dinner with John, his wife Vera Mae, and the four young men. Six months later I visited Mendenhall, MS, John's first ministry headquarters, the center for several practical experiments to economically empower poor African Americans: co-op housing, a credit union, a co-op low-cost clothing store.

John was not in town, but his protégé, Dolphus Weary, was, so I interviewed him as we walked through the framework of a medical center being built. During that time Rita went door to door with Rosie, Dolphus's wife, selling baked goods. The stories I developed from that interview I integrated into the student lessons I was writing for Urban Ministries, into an article for Sunday Digest, and into an article I wrote for Christian Service Brigade's leadership publication. My strategy had become to go for multiple uses of the research done.

## An Article that Opened Doors to Whitey

John Perkins later showed up in Chicago, so I invited the editorial team at Moody Magazine to have coffee with him. They then agreed to let me write a profile on John for the magazine. Two years after the article appeared, John invited me to become a charter member of his national Board of Servants because, he said, "Your article opened the door for white Christians to support our ministry to the poor African Americans in Jackson, MS."

For 20 years I provided encouragement and training for the Voice of Calvary Ministries' writing team when at board meetings, participated in workdays—and spent hours listening to African American leaders discuss the problems they had working with national Christian organizations. They provided an in-depth look at racial discrimination in evangelical organizations as young African American men graduated from Christian colleges or secular universities. After 20 years I was the sole charter member of that first Board of Servants and the only white man left, so many God Moments later I thankfully let another local African American leader take my place.

## The Daunting Backlog in Reference Books

Meanwhile I faced a challenge at Moody Press. Dr. Howard Vos had become a part-time academic editor for Moody Press in the 1960s and started numerous reference book projects. When he moved to King's College in

Briarcliffe, NY he moved into an advisory role, but left behind numerous unfinished projects. Peter Gunther, as director of Moody Press, called me in and promised his strong support to get the reference books completed.

James Matheson, the new academic editor, and I worked together to get the Wycliffe Bible Commentary, Wycliffe Encyclopedia, Old Testament Theological Dictionary back on track. When he left we engaged Dave Douglass, who was more of a desk editor, to provide hands-on editing. Peter Gunther appointed me the chair of the academic committee, a group of professors from Moody, Wheaton College, and Trinity College and Seminary. Eight months of the year we met to discuss which biblically-based textbooks and collateral texts were needed.

Initially, Jim Matheson and I visited colleges and seminaries, sponsoring lunches for professors interested in writing books—and then meeting one-on-one with those with specific book projects. Every year my tour of colleges and seminaries surfaced new textbook and collateral texts ideas, which were run by the Textbook Committee. In time all the projects begun by Dr. Vos were completed and published, along with five or six textbook-related books by leading scholars every year.

## An Inductive Bible Study Genius

One of the most fascinating inductive Bible study series Moody Press published came from the Bible-infused mind of Dr. Irving Jensen, Bible professor at Bryan College in

Tennessee. The goal was to develop usable personal and group inductive Bible studies for every book of the Bible. As Dr. Jensen finished the manuscript for a book, it would be turned over to our designer, who prepared the detailed layout of the studies. Later we had Dr. Jensen write the textbooks *Survey of the Old Testament* and *Survey of the New Testament,* both of which had a strong acceptance in the market. Working with a Moody faculty member, the designer and Dr. Jensen developed overhead transparency study aids for teachers, like biblical maps and charts of historical periods.

While not clearly recognized by the Institute's administration, as editors we believed all of this reference book, textbook, and Bible study material represented an extension of the educational purpose of Moody Bible Institute. All over the country students and small groups were studying books representing the theological/biblical position of the Institute. Sadly, when in 1978 Peter Gunther was moved from his position, like his good friend Kenneth Taylor had been 16 years earlier, five key Moody Press staff left for other positions and that mission fell by the wayside. Where I landed is a story for another chapter, but first I must tell of another God Moment that made Moody Press a Bible publisher of note, a ministry still being carried on today.

# 8

## Helping Moody Press Get into Bibles

My first introduction to the Bible part in Moody Bible Institute came when I became selling floor supervisor of Moody Bookstore in the fall of 1960. Faculty taught Bible courses, so we carried their class notes for students, some of them still reproduced in mimeograph form. But Moody Press had also published *Wuest's New Testament*, an early attempt at giving Greek verbs their due in the English version of the New Testament. As a member of the editorial committee, I was also involved in re-publishing the *Century New Testament,* which never took hold with Bible readers because its original release date had been about 60 years earlier.

We did sell a lot of Bibles to customers, especially evening school students, many of which bought them on a layaway plan, a dollar a week. The one Bible we had to keep under the counter and sell only when it was requested, was the recently released Revised Standard Version. This was being denounced as a "liberal translation" by leading conservative pastors supporting MBI. For me, the irony was that the prize I won five years earlier selling the Bible college yearbooks—which had landed me on the front porch of the man who hired me as denominational weekly editor—was a *Revised Standard Version* of the Bible. No doubt God was amused at the irony of me now selling it surreptitiously.

## The Power of the Bible Story

One of our children's Bible story books in the bookstore had also been Kenneth Taylor's *The Bible in Pictures for Little Eyes,* a bestseller in 1960 and still available in several languages and new packaging. I knew its power in the life of preschoolers from an experience with our daughter, Carol, when she was four. She awakened screaming, "The flybutter. The flybutter." We tried to calm her down, even putting her in the bed between Rita and me, but she would not stop screaming. So Rita took her into the bathroom, put on the lights, and started reading the stories and pointing to the pictures in *The Bible in Pictures for Little Eyes.* In time Carol calmed down from the powerful nightmare of a giant butterfly chasing her, and we were able to put her in her bed, though one of us had to stay with her until she fell asleep.

A true God Moment came when as editor at Moody Press I began signing numerous translation rights contracts that gave a British print packager, Angus Hudson, rights to develop multi-language print orders for *The Bible in Pictures for Little Eyes.* His approach was to assemble orders for a variety of languages, then initially print only the full color pictures in *The Bible in Pictures for Little Eyes,* enough for all languages. Then he'd print the stories in various translations in black type. The process dramatically reduced the printing cost per book for publishers in many different countries, including some countries behind the Iron Curtain.

What also made it possible was that the copies for publishers behind the Iron Curtain were financed by Moody Literature Mission, which was headed by Kenneth Taylor for many years—and later Peter Gunther. In the 1950s and early 1960s the two traveled together to Third World countries to encourage the development of book and magazine publishing—and the opening of Christian bookstores. Moody Literature Mission also placed libraries of 15 mass paperback books published by Moody Press with elementary students in public schools all over the southeast and some other states where school superintendents would permit each child in selected classrooms to receive the 15-book package of Christian storybooks. These Christian story books' influence in communities all over Appalachia has never been studied, but I'm thinking it was real.

## A New Era in Bible Publishing at Moody

*The Living Bible* and other more contemporary translations were challenging the supremacy of the several hundred years old King James Version of the Bible. As a child, as a high school student in a private Mennonite high school, and as a student at the Mennonite Brethren Bible Institute, I had memorized a lot of Bible verses in the King James Version. I was comfortable reading it, but the Jesus Revolution had brought many into Christianity for whom the King James Version was largely incomprehensible. Even a seminary grad like Dr. Kenneth N. Taylor found it hard to read and digest, so he did his own translation, *The Living Bible*.

The Lockman Foundation, originally funded and headed by Dewey Lockman, was established to provide the Bible in a variety of overseas translations based on the most reliable Hebrew and Greek texts. But then they funded an English translation they called the *New American Standard Bible* (NASB). The goal became to develop a new translation faithful to the original Hebrew and Greek for personal Bible study and preaching, but still more understandable than the King James Version.

My next God Moment came when Peter Gunther, our director at Moody Press, asked me to attempt to negotiate a non-exclusive publishing contract for the NASB with The Lockman Foundation. Word in the industry was that several publishers were hoping to work out an exclusive publishing contract and were finding Lockman's board more interested in non-exclusive contracts, hoping to see wider use with several publishers promoting the NASB.

By then I knew that I enjoyed negotiations, so I was delighted to accept the assignment. I flew out to California and met with Robert G. Lambeth of The Lockman Foundation and initiated discussions to gain Moody Press non-exclusive publishing rights. I reported back to Peter Gunther and we developed an approach that resulted in a contract for Moody to publish the NASB Bible in a variety of bindings and specialized uses. Without the Moody Press team realizing it, this move into Bible publishing would soon turn Moody Press into not only a one Bible publishing house, but one with specialty Bibles.

## A Breakthrough God Moment

The next God Moment came unexpectedly at a Christian Booksellers Conference in Dallas, TX in the mid-70s. I was pulled behind a wall at our exhibit by Dr. Charles Ryrie, a professor at the Dallas Theological Seminary and Moody Press author. Dr. Ryrie revealed that he had signed a contract with World Bible Publishing for a *Ryrie Study Bible,* but that the publishing deadline in the contract had not been met. He feared the project was mired in interminable delays and was ready to cancel the contract. Might Moody Press be interested in taking over the project, since his notes for the

New Testament were already completed.

I stood in stunned disbelief. A *Ryrie Study Bible* for Moody Press? Wow, that would be a coup, since Dr. Ryrie had the credentials and teaching experience to deliver notes that a majority of Bible students would accept. Certainly his eschatological views would raise hackles among mid- and post-millenialists, but eschatology was not going to be the main thrust of the Ryrie notes. I quickly came alive and promised to take it up with Peter Gunther and the rest of the executive team. Several weeks later my boss and I met with Dr. Ryrie in a VIP lounge at O'Hare Airport and Peter Gunther and Dr. Ryrie signed the contracts that portended a new era in Bible publishing for Moody Press.

The Moody team decided we needed a simultaneous release as the *King James Ryrie Study Bible* and the *NASB Ryrie Study Bible*. The total cost, including the first printing, was estimated at one million dollars, money loaned to Moody Press by the Institute from its foundation.

## A Mammoth Undertaking

Not surprisingly, this proved to be a mammoth undertaking. David Douglas, as textbook editor, got the job of proofreading. I had noticed an announcement in *Publishers Weekly* about a type designer working with books. I contacted him and we agreed to engage him. He was a charm to work with and delivered a type design and layout we loved. The typesetting for the NASB had been done in a Philadelphia type house, so I negotiated with Robert Lambert at Lockman Foundation to gain access to it for the Ryrie Study Bible.

Howard Fisher, our production manager, evaluated the printing estimates and settled on a printer who could also attach the leather and imitation leather covers. Many executive team meetings later the Ryrie Study Bible rolled off the presses. Now it was up to the publicity and advertising department to get out the message—and the marketing department to prep the salesmen to sell it into the bookstores and special markets. To the best of my knowledge, it was launched in the spring of 1978, if my copy with a 1978 copyright date can be trusted. Eventually, years after I left Moody Press, the NIV version of the Ryrie Study Bible was added. What God had begun in the mind and heart of Dr. Charles Ryrie became THE study Bible for millions.

Yet more than reference books and Bibles were rolling off the press with a Moody Press imprint. In my next installment I'll try to introduce you to some of the wonderful men and women writers I got to introduce to the Editorial Committee, sometimes fight for, and see change the world Christians lived and witnessed in.

# 9

## Two God-Sent Authors

When God brought me to Moody Press in 1970 the editorial department had been without an acquisitions' editor/team leader for two years. Peter Gunther had worked hard to keep the ship afloat, and a reasonably strong backlist had kept sales going. The copy editing and proof-reading team led by Gloria Most worked hard to maintain quality control. My assignment was to breathe new life into the acquisitions process. Fortunately, my eighteen months as manuscript evaluations editor and member of the editorial committee under Ken Taylor gave me a running start.

Peter Gunther quickly introduced me to an acquisition that needed editorial work. Fellow Canadian Philip Keller's biography of an itinerant western Canadian evangelist/

church planter called for extensive editorial work. The result pleased the author so much he brought us *A Layman Looks at the Lord's Prayer* after Zondervan turned it down because "books on the Lord's Prayer do not sell." They did it despite the fact that *A Shepherd Looks at Psalm 23* was starting to climb in sales at Zondervan. For us, *A Layman Looks at the Lord's Prayer* became a God moment.

Billy Graham's "Hour of Decision" had already demonstrated that book hungry listeners would become solid financial contributors if they could get a Billy Graham recommended book in return. The first major breakthrough came for the Graham team when they offered Kenneth N. Taylor's *Living Letters* and a reported 500,000 copies entered homes across the nation. That resulted in significant sales through bookstores and prepared the way for the acceptance of *The Living Bible.*

## A God-Initiated Opportunity

The Moody Press marketing team presented *A Layman Looks at the Lord's Prayer* to the Graham team and they accepted it for a radio giveaway. It got an amazing reception, with several hundred thousand copies being sent to homes as a giveaway. Sales through the Graham office, coupled with Moody Press sales, totaled 70,000, a most acceptable result for a book turned down by a major publisher.

A side note. Marketing departments understandably go by what I call "conventional wisdom," which represents their previous experience with booksellers. What it may not take into consideration is the uniqueness of an author's second book. Even though an editorial department may love that second book, it rarely is able to overcome the conventional wisdom of marketing people that sales of the first book determine a second book's future.

Take for example Max Lucado's first book, published by Tyndale House when story-oriented Christian living books had not yet been introduced to the evangelical market, even though several "liberal" pastors had successfully written them for the secular market. When Lucado's first book did not sell well, the team at Tyndale followed conventional wisdom and turned down his second book. John Van Diest at Multnomah Press took it on. Multnomah, or the author, titled it *No Wonder They Called Him the Savior*—and after several hundred thousand copies had been sold through Christian bookstores a writer-star had been introduced. At one point there were at least four Max Lucado books among the top 10 bestsellers in the Christian market.

## A Strategic Acquisition

Meanwhile a young Canadian pastor at Edgewater Baptist Church in Chicago had written a Master's thesis on the new morality introduced by Bishop Robinson in England. The Rev. Erwin Lutzer brought a popularized version of it to me at Moody Press to see if we'd publish it.

I knew we were on the downside of the bell curve in interest in the New Morality, so sales might fail to reach acceptable numbers, but I was more interested in the next books by the Rev. Erwin Lutzer. The editorial committee accepted my logic and we published it, achieving sales of about 5,000, for us quite acceptable for a first book author.

The Rev. Erwin Lutzer's second book, *How in This World Can I Be Holy* sold much better. His third book, *Failure: The Back Door to Success,* a title I gave it, sold 20,000 the first year and became a solid backlist seller.

Along the way the Rev. Lutzer gained his doctorate and became a faculty member at Moody Bible Institute. In one of his classes five students came to him and admitted to homosexual desires and asked for help in dealing with them. His counseling with them resulted in a book on dealing with addictive desire/behavior as a Christian—and it became the last Lutzer manuscript I processed at Moody Press. While it was completed, it had not yet been put under contract when the Lord moved me to Christian Herald Association (Moody Press practice was not to put a book under contract until an acceptable manuscript was delivered).

Dr. Lutzer took his book manuscript to Victor Books at Scripture Press, who titled it *How to Say No to a Stubborn Habit* and reports were that Victor Books sold 100,000 the first year—and it kept on selling for decades. It illustrated the long-term effects of letting an acquisitions editor get away in an executive upheaval—an event referred to in an earlier chapter. In a later I'll recount the obvious God Moments in my decision-making process in my moves from publishing house to another publishing house.

## A Writer's Dream Opportunity

Moody Memorial Church became Dr. Lutzer's new opportunity when he became the successor to Dr. Warren Wiersbe as senior pastor. As pastor at Edgewater Baptist Church his practice had been to set aside four o'clock Sunday afternoon to rewrite his morning's sermon as a chapter in his next book. His Moody Church responsibilities, which included morning and evening sermons and a radio program, eventually changed that pattern. He invited me to take a sermon series and transform it into book form. One of them became *When a Good Man Falls* and featured how God dealt with the fall into sin by well-known biblical personalities. Victor Books at Scripture Press released it almost a year before Jim Bakker's fall from grace.

A second God Moment came when as vice president of books and book clubs at Christian Herald Association I participated in a writers' conference in Wheaton, IL. Invited by Dr. Lutzer for dinner on Saturday evening of Memorial Day weekend, I arrived at Moody Bible Institute and was standing at the elevator when a radio staff member, Dave McCallister, stepped off the elevator and said to me, "Have you heard about the plane crash at O'Hare Airport?" I had not—and when I learned what flight had crashed I realized I had been scheduled to take that flight to Los Angeles and had canceled it in favor of dinner with the Lutzers. Truly a God Moment.

## A God Moment on a Train

We were hanging on to the straps in a full commuter train out to the Lutzers' suburb when Dr. Lutzer asked me, "Stobbe, what theme should I preach on for our next book?" Instantly the Lord gave me the topic, "Managing Your Emotions." His quick response was, "I'll do it." That book became a perennial seller, partially because the local Christian television station had Dr. Lutzer deliver a series of messages on the topic.

On another occasion Dr. Lutzer had been invited as main speaker at the Mount Hermon Christian Writer's Conference. We were sitting on a bench on the grounds when he turned to me and again asked, "What theme should I preach on?" Our discussion led to another book that had a message for believers struggling with issues like forgiveness. Illustrations came from his counseling ministry with Christians living in a new housing development near the church.

Dr. Lutzer retired from his role as pastor of Moody Memorial Church in 2016, having served the church for more than 35 years, longer than any previous pastor. God has used him in marvelous ways to revive the church, in a widespread revival movement, as a radio and conference speaker and as author of numerous important books.

The next chapter will reveal how God connected me with two interesting Jewish converts to Christianity, authors who represented major God Moment opportunities.

# 10

## My Jewish Connections

What happens when an innovative evangelistic product offends the sensibilities of influential people? In the late 1960s the editorial team at Moody Press became an active proponent of a creative evangelistic and discipling tool, a magazine they called *Emit,* Time spelled backwards. It purported to have been published during the last year or so of Jesus' life, including news reports on Jesus' trial, crucifixion, and resurrection. After it was released to bookstores, it so offended an influential, very conservative leader that he descended on Moody's president and demanded *Emit* be killed and all copies destroyed. During the uproar both the editor and the advertising manager resigned—opening the door for my hiring as editor two years later. Personal taste set back the missions program of Moody Press for two years.

Several years after I became editor at Moody Press I discovered an amazing evangelistic tract series called *Broadsides,* developed by an extraordinarily creative team at Jews for Jesus. As one who had handed out many tracts at street corners, in our local hospital, and going door to door in communities where I co-led Vacation Bible Schools, I was intrigued. As far as I was concerned, the broadsides should not be restricted to street evangelism by Jews for Jesus missionaries, so I presented them to the editorial committee.

## An Evangelistic Project Aborted

I received the go-ahead and negotiated the rights to eight *Broadsides.* While they were on the press the same conservative leader who had blasted *Emit* visited the printer and in the press room saw the broadsides coming off the press. Outraged, he took samples and quickly headed for the office of Moody Bible Institute's president, who at one time had been a chalk-talk evangelist. He called my boss, Peter Gunther, and insisted the *Broadsides* were not well enough drawn to represent the Institute through Moody Press. Rather than trash them, Moody Press gave them to Moody Literature Mission, which distributed them to evangelistic organizations, thus not "sullying" the reputation of Moody by their sales through bookstores worldwide.

My second encounter with a Jewish missionary activist was at the Student Expo sponsored by Campus Crusade for Christ in Dallas, TX in 1972. I came out of the hotel I was staying in one evening to a unique sight. Across the street marched an overalls-clad, somewhat portly individual, in front of a bar featuring scantily-clad women as their attraction, handing out tracts to patrons entering the bar. My journalism instincts kicked in and I crossed the street to more closely observe this phenomenon. I introduced myself to the street missionary, only to discover it was Moishe Rosen, the president of Jews for Jesus.

## Sharing Your Faith Books

Several years later Moody Press was publishing a series of books on sharing your faith with people groups usually considered hard to reach with the message of Christ's love. Not surprisingly, I approached Moishe Rosen about writing a book on *How to Share Your Faith with a Jew.* He gladly agreed to do it and the book was added to a series on sharing your faith with people of a variety of faith positions.

Another of those "sharing your faith" books was by a British missionary with 50 years of ministry to Muslims in North Africa. We had it evaluated by missionaries working with Muslims in several countries in the Indian sub-continent and the Far East—and all agreed it deserved to be published. Marketing remained unconvinced there was a large enough market, projecting sales of possibly 3,000 copies. I researched the potential and reported there were at least two million Muslims in the United States at that time. My boss backed me up and we released the book *How to Share Your Faith with a Muslim,* with sales promptly taking off and 8,000 the first year getting into the hands of Christians eager to reach the Muslim population with the message of Jesus' love for them.

Back to my Jewish connection. A couple of years later we had the opportunity of working with Ceil Rosen, Moishe's wife, on a book. As I remember it, it was a book on the Passover. We released a second book by Ceil Rosen. Fifteen years later Jews for Jesus wanted a book to offer Jewish responders to an ad in major daily newspapers during Operation Desert Storm. By this time I was president of Here's Life Publishers and he approached me about what is called an instant book. We got him a writer willing to interview Moishe, do biblical prophetic research, and write a book in two weeks, which Here's Life editors tackled chapter by chapter as it was submitted. As I remember it, the book came off the press six weeks after being assigned to the writer.

## A Remarkable Encounter

Another of my more remarkable God Moments came at the Dallas, Texas Student Expo of Campus Crusade for Christ. With some time on my hands I wandered over to Crusade's press tent, seemingly deserted at the time—until I saw a bearded younger man who definitely looked Jewish wandering around in the tent. I approached him and introduced myself. He gave me his name, Zola Levitt, and I knew my suspicion was confirmed.

Zola revealed he had been an agnostic all his adult life

and had been a believer in Yeshua as the Messiah only six months. He was trying to find his way in this new world, the evangelical Christian community.

My new friend's story revealed one God Moment after another. He had been attending a Metropolitan Opera regional contest at the University of Indiana as editor of the university's daily newspaper when his eyes fell on the most gorgeous woman he had ever seen. He told the friend next to him to hold his seat while he sauntered over and invited the young woman for coffee. Very reluctantly she agreed.

Zola's agnostic mindset took a hit when this beautiful young woman started sharing her faith in Jesus the Messiah with him—unknown to him, she was a trained Campus Crusade witness. He was so smitten by her he still asked her for a date—and during dates over six weeks she never wavered in her witnessing to the reality that Jesus was the Messiah. He broke off the relationship, but could not get her out of his mind, so he renewed the dating relationship. She invited him to visit her home and church, where he heard another clear message of salvation in Christ Jesus. That night he told Jesus, "If you are real, show me." God invaded his life in such a powerful way he knew Jesus was real right now and loved him. He eventually married the young woman who had through the leading of the Holy Spirit totally ruined his agnostic belief system.

Zola showed up in my office within the next year with a book idea. We ended up publishing eight books by him, all the way from a book on touring Israel to a book on witnessing to his childhood friend through a series of letters.

When he teamed up with Tom McCall, an American Board of Missions to the Jews staff member, for a book on the Third Temple, eventually entitled *Satan in the Sanctuary*, Moody had a genuine bestseller. They teamed up as well for *The Coming Russian Invasion of Israel,* which also sold at the level of a bestseller. Years later during Desert Storm they updated the book and it had a second run as a Moody Press book.

## Knowing When to Compromise

Zola was a firm, confident author to work with. After all, he had conducted operas, led a symphony orchestra, played an oboe and the French horn at a professional level—and been a daily newspaper reporter. He knew exactly what he wanted—and early on that clashed with our conservative managing editor. On his first book with us he was aghast that the editor had strictly followed the *Chicago Manual of Style* and eliminated all his contractions and other indicators of his personal style. After all, he had followed the AP Manual of Style.

Our editor refused to budge even though she was attending a Messianic Fellowship—if one author got away with it, others could as well, was her rationalization. But Zola also refused to back down—he wanted an informal style that he believed appealed to his readers. It seemed Moody Press was about to lose a valuable acquisition—and possibly a series of books—so I asked for the galley proof. With a red pen I gave him most of what he asked for. We saved a valuable contributor to our bottom line—and thereby also contributed to Zola launching an international Bible teaching ministry.

Zola was remarkably creative. He would dress in period clothing, stand in front of a biblical site in the Mideast, and have movie cameras rolling as he presented his biblical message. Then he put them on television. He wrote, composed, and directed in live performances his cantata, gave tours of Israel, building a television ministry that eventually reached every state in the nation—and attracted an international following. The sale of his books, the tours he led to Israel, his speaking engagements, provided a source of income that supported his television ministry and relieved him of constant appeals for financial support.

The next chapter will tackle a range of author and work experiences at Moody Press that created an environment leading to a far-reaching decision based on a God Moment.

# 11

## Entering the World of Book Clubs

When you are leaving a publisher for another one, what kind of farewell should you expect? I was obviously not going to a competitor of Moody Press, since the Christian Herald Association was known for its magazine and its book clubs, not its book publishing program. Despite that it came as quite a surprise when I was invited to have lunch with Dr. George Sweeting, president of Moody Bible Institute. Even though I had been acquiring editor for several of his books, I wondered what was on his agenda.

We met in a private dining area reserved for meetings of special people. After prayer we tackled our meal and began small talk. Then I discovered Dr. Sweeting's agenda. As best I remember it he said, "I understand why you are leaving. If I were you I would also be leaving." I was stunned. He explained that he disagreed with the decisions made by the Institute executives regarding Moody Press, but that as their president he felt duty bound to support the executives' decisions. He wished me Godspeed and gave me his blessing as I moved on to my new opportunity at Christian Herald Association. His taking the time to have lunch with me gave me a new level of respect for him. What he as a former pastor would have appreciated is that my transition to Christian Herald would put us in a place where God could use my wife and me in an exciting new church adventure.

## God's Moment in Finding a Home

Our search for a new home with a large living room for hospitality landed us in Danbury, CT, then already a high-tech center and home to executives commuting by rail to New York. Shortly after we arrived, an international company, Union Carbide, moved its headquarters to Danbury, bringing thousands of workers with them.

We had attended a local church for several months when in another God Moment, Rita was told about Black Rock Congregational Church in Fairfield, CT—and we began driving 21 miles to it. While we quickly got involved in leadership positions in Christian education and music, our home came alive with social events and a Bible study. Two years later a phone call from the chair of the elder board changed our focus.

"We know you have wanted us to start a new church in

Danbury. Our church office has had five calls from families in Danbury asking us to begin a daughter church there. Would you get these families together to check them out?"

## God's Reason for Being in Danbury

He did not know that I had a degree in pastoral theology, that I had been acting pastor, done a lot of pulpit supply, had been on several elder boards. All that experience now became a God Moment as we began a Sunday evening Bible study in our home. Several months later the group, which contained executives in leading companies, including a vice president at Union Carbide, approached the Black Rock Congregational Church elder board for permission to organize as a daughter church. They not only approved the move, they let us have three elders as representatives of the sponsoring church. We eventually presented our plans to the congregation at Black Rock Congregational Church and received a near unanimous vote in favor of completing the organizational process.

The leadership team projected the new church would grow to 125 members in five years. Yet the first Sunday morning meeting in a Ramada Inn brought out a full house, 125 active Christians—and five months later the church had grown to 200 and had a full-time pastor. Today the church has 2400 or more in several services and five church plants. It was the key church in helping parents of children killed at the Sandy Hook School massacre. The church brought in author Philip Yancey because of the book he had written on grief. God used him and the church in tackling the deep grief of those parents.

Unfortunately, Rita and I were not part of that growth because an unexpected job change sent us to California.

## A Learning Experience

Meanwhile I was commuting 35 miles to Christian Herald Association offices in Chappaqua, NY. The editors and design team were doing a great job of selecting books for The Christian Herald Family Bookshelf and two subsidiary book clubs in the heart of America, as well as Christian Women's Book Club. My focus turned to my other assignment, expanding the book list of the small book publishing arm, when I learned a most important publishing lesson.

Before I had arrived, the leadership had been ecstatic over acquiring the memoir of the wife of the treasury secretary in the government of President Jimmy Carter. It had been released to the public and seemed destined to be a bestseller when the unthinkable happened. The author's husband was involved in a scandal and released by the president. Just as I arrived the wife's book was being boxed up and returned by booksellers. More than 35,000 books showed up at the warehouse and had to be destroyed. This confirmed a truth I had been told by a British book packager, Angus Hudson, who said, "It's not how many books you sell, but how many books are returned by booksellers that determine profitability."

The reality of that came alive soon after I joined Here's Life Publishers, when we released a book by Richard Nixon's personal lawyer. He had come to faith in Christ after Watergate, like Chuck Colson. Orders came in thick and fast—only to result in 38,000 coming back in returns when the author only preached when on radio or TV instead of telling what it was like to be a part of the Watergate scandal. This confirmed that radio is an entertainment media with a voracious appetite for people's unusual experiences, with little interest in authors who prefer preaching to telling stories.

## A Strange Meeting

Early on at Christian Herald Association I had a surprise—another strange meeting. A long-term executive of the Christian Herald Association invited me to accompany him to New York City, where we were ushered into the posh offices of a key executive and a major player in the finance world. He happened to be Chairman of the Board of Christian Herald Association. After small talk he said the board was considering releasing the president of Christian Herald Association. Did I consider myself prepared to take that position?

I had had a similar meeting with an executive vice president and the head of personnel when I was hired for Moody Press—and nothing had come of that, so I was wary. This time I was asked to report instances of malfeasance that could present an opportunity to replace Christian

Herald's president. I listened but in my heart I knew I could never do that. Rat on a new boss who had bent over backwards to hire me? I left that meeting knowing I absolutely could not do that.

I thoroughly enjoyed my relationships with staff I worked with. We offered a main selection and a secondary selection 15 times a year in both the Family Bookshelf and Christian Women's Book Club. Members who signed up received four free books. Then we prepared a promo for two books that members could purchase at a discounted price, but since we were a negative option book club, they had to respond negatively to the promo, or we mailed them the two selections with an invoice. Fifty percent of our selections were overtly Christian books licensed from publishers and fifty percent were "clean" selections from general publishers, with a lot of them coming from regional publishers.

One of my major contributions was a discovery at the post office in Washington, DC that as a Christian book club we could ship our books at a reduced rate—over the next year it saved us $125,000, which significantly increased our net profit.

One of my perks was to visit Mont Lawn summer camp for inner city children operated by the Association in the Pocono Mountains. They also had a full-time person following up the children during the rest of the year. Another perk was to occasionally visit The Bowery, the New York City rescue mission operated by the Association. More than 100 years old, it attracted volunteers from as far away as Mennonite country in Pennsylvania. When the Mennonites came, they always brought a truckload of produce for the kitchen.

## Time for Another God Moment

While the Family Bookshelf was the key income producer, the Christian Women's Book Club failed to reach profitability—nor did the book publishing enterprise, even though we acquired numerous books by leading authors. We had not reached what every business needs to reach, a critical mass. One book we had a chance of acquiring could have put us on the map in publishing—Kevin Leman's *Sex Begins in the Kitchen.* I was laughed at by the team when I presented it and forced to turn it down, so Dr. Leman went with Regal Books and it sold hundreds of thousands of copies. Eight years later one book, *Building Your Mate's Self-Esteem,* by Dennis Rainey, put us at Here's Life Publishers on the road to profitability—but that story is for a later chapter.

The real loser at Christian Herald Association was the *Christian Herald Magazine,* for which we had celebrated 100 years of publishing soon after I got there. The magazine would become a casualty of bad publishing decisions and of the encroaching digital age. These factors—and a change of ownership at our printer/distributor—combined to make it necessary to sell off something. The book program was selected for that.

Our president felt I was valuable enough to package me

with the book program as sales bait. I knew that would not work, so realized God would have to open up another door. An editor I had used as a writer of books turned out to be God's tool to open a surprising door that triggered a move across country to southern California. The next chapter will get us into a remarkably difficult but interesting publishing period for me, where God Moments abounded—and a fascinating opportunity for my wife, Rita, emerged in another God Moment.

# 12

## Getting Settled in California

Two questions come to mind when thinking back to our move from Connecticut to Southern California in 1982.

 What does a couple leave behind when forced to make a major move? What unexpected consequences can imperil a successful transition?

Let's tackle the first question in this installment. One word provides an answer to the first question: memories. While the founding of a church in our home was undoubtedly the most exciting, a less momentous one remains vivid after 39 years. In Danbury our home stood on a triangle of land extending into a small pond that at one time had provided frogs for New York eateries in summer and ice blocks for iceboxes in winter. The frogs were basically gone, with turtles sitting on every rock protruding above the water. Winter ice, on the other hand, provided an attractive surface for skaters, with hockey games going on simultaneously on three sides of our home. In fact, our first winter was so cold the pond froze to the bottom.

I was feeding 32 ducks who had not migrated with corn the previous owner had left behind, but I had to finally give up chopping a hole in the ice so they could have water. During spring melt ice piling up revealed large catfish still encased in ice. Our fears that we would later have the horrible smell of decaying fish were allayed when dozens of seagulls arrived and cleared all the fish out of the melting ice.

A God Moment with huge implications occurred when a friend at a women's gathering told Rita about a church 21 miles down Black Rock Turnpike. Our experiences at Black Rock Congregational Church left us with many God Moments. Soon after we began attending services an adult class leader moved—and I was invited to take his place. The class members loved Bible discussions, so I'd typically arrive with only questions as my notes. Several months later I was asked to become chair of the Christian Ed Committee and participated in planning for significant enhancements to the church. Rita was asked to become chair of the Music Committee. She left her mark not only in occasionally leading the choir but also in negotiating moving of the choir to behind the pastor from one side of the sanctuary. She also spearheaded fun parties at our house and the church for members looking for relationship building opportunities. These involvements smoothed the way for us helping plan a new church for Danbury.

## Hello California!

A writer I had formerly published provided the God Moment that resulted in a telephone call inviting me to come for an interview for editorial director of Here's Life Publishers. We arrived for our interview at the for-profit subsidiary of Campus Crusade for Christ International on December 18—and by Dec. 23 knew what my next field of ministry would be. My assignment was to ramp up the acquisition of books that would move the book publisher into profitability and provide guidance for a young but competent editor, John Carvalho, of *Athletes in Action Magazine.*

But first we had to sell our Danbury home and acquire one reasonably close to the office. But how do you sell or buy a house when the mortgage rate is 18 percent? God provided a couple who rented our home with option to buy—and we moved into a former show home at a new development with a similar arrangement. Six months later we knew we would have to abandon the home because noise from engines at Norton Airbase revving up at four in the morning bounced off the neighbor's house into our bedroom. In addition, the kitchen was located in the southwest corner and was the hotbox of the house despite air-conditioning. We discovered our pastor was looking to rent their house nearby, so we moved into it.

For one year that house became home to a lively Bible study group, including a key executive at Mission Aviation International, a member of a government intelligence unit whose secrets were never divulged, several veteran Christians and one seeker. If you've never been part of group that put its loving arms around a recently divorced spiritual seeker, try it. When she desperately needed encouragement, the group gave it. When her car broke down, she was helped. And when the God Moment arrived when she accepted Jesus as her Savior, we all rejoiced.

A God Moment a year later developed slowly. Rita went house hunting with a Christian realtor, seeing a home she really liked but we felt we could not afford. Months later we were told the house we were renting was being sold. Rita remembered her brother saying, "Make a ridiculous offer and go from there," so we approached the realtor about the house Rita liked, an estate sale. Reluctantly, she agreed to present our offer of $25,000 less than the listed price, with the two married children carrying the mortgage at 10 percent, well below the going rate. The counter-offer was what we had hoped for. We praised the Lord, but we had no down payment, since our Danbury home had not yet sold. In another God Moment, the realtor volunteered to provide a bridge loan. Several months later our Danbury property was purchased and the bridge loan repaid. Now we faced significant renovation, accomplished over five years.

## Staff Needs for New Ministry Tools

Here's Life Publishers served several constituencies. One was the staff of Campus Crusade for Christ, with the evangelism and discipleship books that staff under Bill Bright's direction had written and used for years. The second constituency was the one developed by Josh McDowell's apologetic campus ministry and youth groups beyond that. The Family Ministry of Dennis Rainey represented the third significant constituency. We also served the high school ministry, the ministry to churches, prison ministry, ministry to athletes and ministry to foreign diplomats in the U.S.

I soon learned college campus ministries were unhappy with the evangelism and discipleship tools written several decades earlier, with some using NavPress materials, some material developed in England. We learned staff at a Texas University were about to embark on writing their own material. In a God Moment, my boss, Dave Orris, engaged a former educational specialist and an editor/writer from Gospel Light Publishing to set up a meeting in Texas with the dissident group.

With Dr. Brown leading the meeting, 20 staff began explaining what they were looking for. Ideas flowed quickly and were put on large sheets taped onto the wall, a form of storyboarding. By the end of the day, we knew what staff was looking for. Over the summer staff from several colleges and universities settled into dorms at Redlands University and, as I remember it, worked for six weeks on new evangelism and discipleship booklets, with the editor/writer transforming suggestions into booklet form. Our job at Here's Life Publishers was to edit and print the booklets in time for the 1983 Christmas event for thousands of college students from all over the U.S. The God Moment came when the new material for evangelism and discipleship was introduced and put in the hands of staff.

For the nine years Here's Life Publishers served Campus staff after that, we heard no complaints, only accolades. After all, campus staff got what they asked for, based on their input. If only more educational material for use in Sunday Schools and youth programs were produced with that much input from end users!!

We discovered another area of discontent. Even though we sold four million copies of *The Four Laws* booklet a year, a growing number of Crusade staff were ordering the British version, *Would You Like to Know God Personally?* Bill Bright shared with me his unhappiness over the growing use of the British version, which he considered too wordy and not as clear as his *The Four Laws* booklet. As a writer I liked the warm spirit of the title and appeal to a personal relationship of the British version, so I set about editing, rewriting the British version. After several consultations with Bill Bright, he was satisfied and approved us printing it. For me, that was a God Moment. Sales soon equaled those of *The Four Laws* and today it is the most used evangelistic tool of CRU (the new name of Campus Crusade for Christ) staff members.

## Capturing Bill Bright's Heart for Evangelism

In interacting with Bill Bright I became aware he badly wanted to write a book on personal evangelism, but nothing had been done about it. I felt that could be a major legacy if done right. I developed a title, *Witnessing without Fear* and prepared a dozen chapter titles, running the approach by Bill Bright. He loved it, but I knew he would never take the time to write it. Asking around at the International School of Theology a faculty member mentioned the name of a former editor at Crusade's magazine, Worldwide Challenge.

Dan Benson agreed to accept the assignment. Bill Bright agreed to give us two days alone with him in his board room. I had developed questions for every chapter designed to elicit stories of successes in personal evangelism, since Dan as former CRU staff had absorbed Bill Bright's teaching on evangelism. We heard about one God Moment after another as Bill Bright regaled us with stories of leading people to faith in Christ. One of his extraordinarily successful approaches on an airplane was to settle in a seat in the economy section and give his seatmate a copy of The Four Spiritual Laws and say something like, "I'd like to discuss this with you after you've read it." He led many taxi drivers from all over the world to faith in

Christ just on a ride from one part of a major city to another.

Our Here's Life Publishers marketing team projected sales of maybe 5,000 copies of *Witnessing without Fear*, since in our experience CRU staff were oral communicators and not active book buyers. I was more hopeful than that, so was delighted when sales totaled 30,000 copies the first year it was offered to the public. Another God Moment came when the book won the Gold Medallion Award for the most outstanding evangelistic book of the year.

More about Bill Bright and his wife Vonette as book authors in the next chapter—and how one of Vonette's books led to a very special writing assignment for me.

# 13

## Tackling a Financial Crisis

How can God turn an overwhelming debt load at a publishing house into a series of God Moments? At Here's Life Publishers we served as a for profit subsidiary of Campus Crusade for Christ, with the chairman of the Board the executive vice-president of Crusade. What I did not realize when I arrived as editorial director was that Here's Life Publishers had been kept afloat by regular draws on a "slush fund" at Crusade, that our losses would be half a million on sales of just over two million the year I arrived.

Our product line consisted basically of Crusade's evangelism and discipleship materials—and Josh McDowell apologetic books, like *Evidence that Demands a Verdict,* easily our bestseller. I put my book acquisitions hat on and began reaching out to possible book authors. But as a small publisher we were not in a position to compete against the much larger publishers, so we published what God gave us in first book authors.

One day the president of Here's Life invited me to join him at lunch, where he told me that over the next year he would prepare me for taking over as president. David Orris kept his word. He left for another publisher mid-year of 1985 and turned leadership over to me—the Board confirmed me after proper vetting.

## Discovering Financial Reality

While this was going on I discovered financial reality. We were hundreds of thousands of dollars in debt to two printers—and had a negative credit rating. Any printer we approached demanded cash with each printing order, but the formerly ready cash from the Crusade "slush fund" was no longer available.

My first of a series of God Moments came when an accounting executive of a large firm was seconded to us. He found our books in good order. Then he suggested he and I visit the printers to whom we were indebted. His background helped us work out a two-year payment plan for each.

Then we tackled what Crusade carried on their books as our indebtedness to them—the withdrawals by the previous president of Here's Life. Working with the Crusade corporate lawyer, we got the Crusade Board to turn the debt into company shares. With that our credit rating dramatically improved and we could get credit with more cost effective printers in the Midwest. We also changed our production manager, who had refused to change to less costly printers for reasons I found out later.

To reduce office and warehouse costs we moved from our own freestanding building into offices in a Crusade office complex, switching to a warehouse/shipping service and ditching our badly programmed computer for fulfilling orders. Wayne Hastings, who I had asked to be executive vice-president, had a background in computer sales.

Through a local computer assembler Wayne got every editor and marketing person a computer on their desk. He found a software developed for small publishers that took only three days to become operational—another God Moment. He got us hooked up by computer with the shipping services of Appalachian Bible Distributors so that at the end of every day we could transmit our orders for next day order picking and shipping. Other software gave our editors the capability to do the page design that is usually a significant cost factor. Pages were transmitted via computer to a laser printer, which delivered pages ready for the printer.

We were now leaders among Christian publishers in initiating desktop publishing, giving us a major cost reduction in book production.

## A Charles Swindoll God Moment

Those actions still did not make us profitable, even with an expanding book list. I was waking up nights at 3:00 a.m. in a cold sweat, facing a most unattractive reality—our publishing house could be forced to declare bankruptcy.

Then God launched another God Moment. Driving to work one morning I heard Charles Swindoll on radio quote Jeremiah 29:11, "For I know the plans that I have for you, declares the Lord, plans for welfare and not for calamity, to give you a future and a hope" (NASB). I met Wayne Hastings arriving at the office

"Did you hear Charles Swindoll read Jeremiah 29:11?" I asked him. He said he had and I invited him to join me in my office. Together we claimed that promise for Here's Life Publishers. At home that evening I opened my Bible to the passage, put it on my prayer chair, knelt and prayed, "Lord, Here's Life Publishers is not mine. It is yours. I turn it all over to you. I am claiming Jeremiah 29:11 for Here's Life Publishers." That night when I woke up I repeated the verse and went back to sleep, as I did often after that.

In his foreknowledge God had already started a series of publishing events that would fulfill the future we believed he had promised us. After years of effort to enlist Dennis Rainey, head of Family Life Ministries of Crusade, as author, it became reality. He and his wife wrote *Building Your Mate's Self-Esteem*. After extensive rewriting, it was accepted as a giveaway on James Dobson's "Focus on the Family" broadcast—and they eventually bought 39,000 copies to give away during the days Dennis was interviewed by Dr. Dobson. Pre-orders had piled up, so that I ordered "All hands on deck" in the shipping area—and I spent hours daily packing books. With Dennis appearing on the radio broadcast of "Focus on the Family," our first year sales totaled over 130,000 copies. We had our first big winner and praised God for his response to Jeremiah 29:11!

**The God Moment in Action**

The following spring we released *A Door of Hope,* by Jan Frank, which sold 16,000 copies the first year, with increased sales in subsequent years. We also released *Roses in December,* by Marilyn Willett Heavilin, a book for parents grieving the loss of a child that sold 25,000 the first year and stayed in print for decades. Both had been turned down by other publishers and were brought to us by Florence Littauer after I had lunch with her and her husband, Fred.

But God had another surprise for us. Since early the previous year Josh McDowell's team and we had been working on books for a massive "Why Wait?" campaign by Josh, focusing on stemming pre-marital sexual activity among Christian teens. As the result of a survey by Josh's team we together developed the book *What I Wish My Parents Knew About My Sexuality,* with Josh as author. Released in May, 1987, it sold 75,000 copies the first year. Then in July we released the centerpiece for his crusade entitled simply *Why Wait?* With Josh as author, it was purchased by "Focus on the Family" for a giveaway, Josh was interviewed on "Focus on the Family," and we sold more than 140,000 copies the first year. Suddenly we were a profitable publisher. And God had delivered on his promise in Jeremiah 29:11.

Around this time we were invited to help Bill Bright write a one-year daily devotional book. Working closely with him was our veteran editor, Jean Bryant. The book had a strong evangelistic and discipling thrust, satisfying a long-standing desire on Bill's part.

## Marriage Secrets Revealed

Next came a request from Bill for a book on marriage, to be written by Bill and Vonette. Our writer and I spent hours interviewing them, digging for realism on what it meant to be an international couple. Stories we heard included a time when the Crusade director for an Indian sub-continent country arrived for a visit. Bill had a special affection for shirts he had bought in South Africa, though Vonette did not particularly care for them, so he went into the closet for one of them. They had not yet been ironed. Vonette was not at home, so he set about ironing one, but only the front and sleeves, since the jacket would cover the rest. The director arrived on a warm day and shocked his host by quickly taking off his jacket. Bill as host had to join his guest, displaying a partially ironed shirt to Vonette's huge embarrassment.

Vonette told us a story Bill would not let us put in the book. They had a serious argument about some phase of reconstruction at the hotel Crusade had purchased as headquarters. Bill was not giving her the attention she felt she deserved in remodeling plans. To end the argument he decided to take off in their car for an appointment. Vonette stormed out after him and placed herself in front of the car—and made her point.

Later we worked with Vonette on her idea for a book entitled *The Greatest Lesson I've Ever Learned,* with chapters contributed by well-known women friends. One of the contributors was Dale Evans Rogers. Our editorial director, Dan Benson, had been a huge admirer of Roy Rogers as a boy and decided we would try for a book by Dale. We met her for lunch and asked her what kind of a book she might like to write.

## The Dale Evans Rogers Opportunity

"I'd like to write a book on humility, because that's in short supply in Hollywood, but no publisher I've given the idea is interested," she replied. In one of those God Moments I asked, "What if we focused on a biblical image, that of God being the potter and we being the clay? Wouldn't that reveal dependence on God, which reflects humility?"

She responded, "I don't know anything about pottery, but if you do, let's do it." What she did not know was that some years earlier Rita and I had lived next to a potter who had her own kiln. Dale signed a contract for the book. When we were sold to Thomas Nelson the contract went to them, as did Dan Benson, our editorial director. When the editorial team at Thomas Nelson reviewed the unfulfilled contracts at Here's Life Publishers, they asked Dan about the Dale Evans Rogers' one. He suggested that since Dale was over 80 and had already had a heart attack, she was not likely to write it, but I was between jobs and could write it with her.

That's how God gave me another God Moment—the delightful experience of spending four two-hour periods interviewing Dale for stories of her life and two hours interviewing Roy Rogers, then interviewing several of their children, plus reading out-of-print Dale books. Then I wrote the book manuscript, including biblical content to make the book suitable for a Bible study, which Dale warmly approved. When Thomas Nelson invited Dale and Roy to their sales conference—they were a huge hit—and the salesmen went out and sold it strongly, achieving sales of 40,000 copies within the first three months and No. 17 on the bestseller list.

In the next chapter I'll reveal more about how Here's Life Publishers furthered the evangelistic ministry of Crusade college staff and Josh's apologetic ministry—and how a Bill Bright ministry desire resulted in the sale of Here's Life Publishers over Board members of Here's Life Publishers' objections.

# 14

## The High Cost of Success

The last chapter introduced the God Moments that transformed Here's Life Publishers from a money-losing struggle into a profitable publishing house, however, as I will reveal later, the cost was higher than anyone anticipated. But before I reveal the details leading to the sale of Here's Life Publishers I'll introduce tools for evangelism and discipleship we published to enhance the ministry of our parent, Campus Crusade for Christ.

In installment 12, I revealed the development and publishing of a successful new series of evangelism follow-up discipling tools for campus ministries—and giving the Four Laws booklet a new title, *Would You Like to Know God Personally?* and friendlier content. I introduced Bill Bright's *Witnessing Without Fear* and Josh's apologetic books. We kept our eyes and ears open for book projects by Crusade staff that would foster the evangelism and discipleship that lie at the heart of their ministry.

## A Disciple Making Book

A God Moment came at Crusade's biennial staff training retreat in Colorado. I met with Chris Adsit, then the national discipling coordinator for Athletes in Action, who had spent four years in discipleship activity with the Navigators. In 1975 Chris had been named all-American in the Decathlon and participated in international competition. As we faced each other over lunch he told me about the amazingly detailed personal discipling chart he had developed and his desire to write a book about personal disciple-making. We agreed a good start would be a 128-page book.

Months later Chris delivered a 500-page manuscript entitled *Personal Disciple-Making.* We wondered who, even the most committed disciple, would read a 500-page book! But since Chris was a key staff member of Crusade, we decided to edit out any "fat" we'd find—with our editing department eventually delivering a 384-page final proof to our production manager.

Our marketing team agreed we'd better put a high price on it, since they expected to sell only 3,000 copies. They had not counted on the impact of 17 endorsements by pastors, staff, and also Dr. Howard Hendricks, nationally-known speaker and professor at Dallas Theological Seminary. That first year our marketing team sold 12,000 copies, quadrupling their prediction, making it a financially successful book—and a ministry many times that of what was expected. Chris tapped into his international connections and added a ministry in South Africa with his book.

## A Student-Oriented Evangelism Tool

Now we had a first-rate how-to book on evangelism and one on personal discipling, plus specialized discipling booklets, but what about a unique evangelism tool for campus ministry? The chairman of our Here's Life Publishing board and executive vice-president of Campus Crusade for Christ, Steve Douglas, approached us with an idea, a book entitled *How to Make Better Grades and Have more Fun.* We engaged a former editorial staff member of Crusade's Worldwide Challenge magazine, Al Janssen, to work with Steve and together they wrote the book.

Steve decided we should put a challenge on the outside back cover. If reading the book and putting its principles into practice did not help high school or college students improve their grades by a full point, we'd return their purchase cost. No takers ever developed, but when a college or university campus team distributed it to new students on campus, inviting them to a meeting, Steve would fly out to address those who turned out. Consistently, 50 percent of those attending made a decision to accept Jesus as Savior. Publishing mission accomplished.

Working with Josh McDowell and a writer he enlisted, Don Stewart, we published a series of four books on cults and world religions that sold very well. We worked with Josh to develop and publish a book on personal Bible study.

## Becoming Part of a Dream

Over the years we faced a number of staff crises and were forced to release several key members if we were to achieve our goal of keeping a godly team together. God then brought some genuinely effective professionals to our staff. We gathered the team on short notice if a prayer concern, like the illness of a staff member, arose. We met every week around God's Word and prayer.

One day we learned that Dr. Bright was thinking of selling us to hopefully raise one million dollars to fulfill his dream of a New Life Center in Moscow. Over a year we had several publishers evaluate our performance and what we might bring to a publisher. Yet none were willing to pay cash at the level Dr. Bright wanted. He contacted Sam Moore, president of Thomas Nelson, and he sent a team to do due diligence, examining our accounting system, our marketing approach, the books we were publishing, our credit rating.

The Thomas Nelson team doing the evaluation assured us we had the cleanest financial books they had seen in some time. They were astonished what our marketing people accomplished with limited promotional dollars, and our desktop publishing approach gave us a significantly lower production cost per book than they were experiencing.

When our board of two Crusade executives and three outside members met, they questioned the wisdom of selling a profitable publishing house producing effective tools for evangelism and discipling, the key ministries of our parent. Objections were over-ridden and the sale made to fulfill our president's dream of a Here's Life center in Moscow.

Now my job was to keep the staff together and gain them a separation bonus based on years of service—which our parent let us provide. Remarkably, only one staff member left before we closed our doors. After 11 years in San Bernardino, Calif., I faced the uncertainty of finding a new job, but God had another few God Moments for me as a writer before I got back into publishing.

## An International Opportunity

Over the years I had developed a good relationship with a Mr. Hui Lin, a Crusade staff member in Singapore who was a remarkable entrepreneur. He had developed a book distribution outlet for Christian publishers in the U.S. and the UK and served staff and Christian bookstores throughout Asia. He approached me about helping him develop Christian book authors in Asia. We agreed on a Friday evening and Saturday all day writers' conference in a suburb of Manila, in the Philippines—and an all-day one on a national holiday in Singapore in the spring of 1992, the year our publishing house was sold to Thomas Nelson.

I arrived in Singapore after visiting a brother and his family doing church planting in Japan. I received a tour of Manila, a truly immense city. I learned that 250 writers had signed up for the conference, but the room could hold only 225. Even then air conditioning could not keep up and by mid-morning Saturday I was feeling weak. During the break I was taken next door and served a cold Mango juice drink that quickly refreshed me. I was interviewed for a local newspaper article and met with seminary faculty that evening, where I experienced one of the rotating power outages because drought had cut down electricity output. After I left, a group of writers organized to encourage one another and put into practice some of what they had learned.

Sunday morning we arrived at the airport to airport controllers on strike. After sitting around all day Mr. Lin and I experienced a God Moment—we were able to board the last flight out of Manila for Singapore. The next day I led 125 Singapore writers in a series of workshops, later meeting several one-on-one to discuss their writing opportunities. A special privilege was addressing a group of Christian booksellers. Sightseeing for a day included a delightful visit to a bird park.

In the next chapter we'll tackle God Moments as a writer before he opened a door to an unusual opportunity as a curriculum managing editor.

# 15

## Does Age Really Matter?

Before I wrap up my 11 years with Here's Life Publishers of Campus Crusade for Christ (now known as CRU), let me reflect on a God Moment with long term impact.

Before I left New England for Here's Life Publishers I helped Gordon College's alumni relations director develop a plan for a Christian writers conference. By the time the conference was held I had moved to California and Here's Life, but I decided to fly back and see what God would do at the conference.

The second night of the conference became a talent night, with writers reading poems, short stories, singing. In the middle of the program a gray-haired woman with a winning smile got up and told a story from her growing up years in a Norwegian immigrant pastor's family. By the time she was halfway through her story I knew I had to meet her. I followed her into the hall and asked, "Do you have any more of these stories?" She smiled demurely and said, "I have a manuscript full of them." I asked to see it and in a God Moment realized I had struck a vein of gold.

Margaret Jensen was the mother of the wife of the dean of Gordon College, Wenham, MA. Her daughter and son-in-law had insisted she come to the conference because they were aware of her story-telling ability. I later discovered she was 67 years old, a retired nurse, who with her pastor husband had moved to Georgia to take on a pastorate. Coming from the north, the Jensens did not have the prejudices of many in the church, so they began collecting clothing and food for African American families living in poverty—and worked to get the children an education. That so scandalized church members and leaders that they finally called a membership meeting to fire the pastor. Before the Jensens went into the church a friend alerted them that there were plans afoot to tar and feather the pastor and ride him out of town. Their advice, "Get out of town as fast as you can." They did. The experience so unnerved and depressed Margaret's husband that he did not take another pastorate.

## The God Moment Continues

I took Margaret's manuscript with me and introduced it to my boss, Dave Orris, and then the editorial committee. They agreed to publish it with the author's title, *First We Have Coffee*. Because I had just come from leading the book club program at Christian Herald Family Bookshelf, I approached the editor, Mary Risley, about making it a selection in the book club. After reading the manuscript for *First We Have Coffee* she agreed to make it a main selection, releasing it to her club just before we released the book to the Christian bookstores. God was gracious and the book club sold more than 20,000 copies and a year later we recognized our sales through bookstores also totaled over 20,000 copies.

What we did not realize at the time was that Margaret Jensen's well of stories never ran dry—and that she would explode on the national scene as a speaker/storyteller. She traveled all over the U.S. telling her stories in liberal and conservative churches, in Catholic churches, to seniors in large churches and senior communities, to the rapt attention of teens. Each year we released another collection of her stories: *Lena, Papa's Place, Violets for Mr. B, A Nail in a Sure Place, The Mending Basket*—and many more. The whole list can be found on amazon.com.

*Lena,* the story of an African American nurse's aide who helped Margaret pray a wayward-son-turned-racist in a Christian college into a loving family man, brought phone calls from all over the country. Families descended on the Jensen's home in North Carolina, arriving unannounced to ask for prayer. After Margaret and Lena spoke to a large Sunday school class in a Methodist church people lined up after the service to have Lena, the African American heroine in the story, pray for them.

## Impact on One Family

In one family where *First We Have Coffee* was read, the Christian mother grieved over a husband resistant to the message of life in Christ—and a son in a drug rehab program. After reading *Lena* she embarked on renewed prayer—and gave her husband the tape of Margaret telling the stories in *Lena* to listen to on his trip to see his son. On the way home he drove onto the breakdown lane, stopped the car, and turned his life over to Jesus Christ. Months went by. One day Margaret was walking in a nearby mall when an oncoming young man called out, "Margaret Jensen!!" She stopped and he approached, saying, "I'm the young man who was in drug rehab and I've become a Christian."

Twenty-five years later I was to remember the amazing sales pattern of all of Margaret Jensen's books when a 25-year-veteran of Emergency Room experiences, Dr. Robert Lesslie, presented his collection of stories over lunch. I took that proposal with me and as agent sent it out. After three editors told me, "Collections of stories don't sell," Harvest House took it on, with sales of his series of Emergency

Room stories, starting with *Angels in the ER,* at well over 360,000 copies as I write this. Sadly, on April 8, 2021, Dr. Robert Lesslie and his wife Barbara and two granddaughters were brutally murdered in their home. His legacy of 10 books lives on.

In the next chapter I'll reveal the God Moments that provided extraordinary writing opportunities after Here's Life Publishers was sold, and I was set adrift with no job in sight.

# 16

## Transition Provides New Opportunities

Despite the seeming tragedy of losing an exciting opportunity as president of Here's Life Publishers in 1992, the Lord kept dropping opportunities my way. In addition to the two books described in the previous installment, I was approached about helping a marriage counselor upgrade his book, *Discovering the Mind of a Woman.* I spent a fascinating weekend interviewing Ken Nair on his and his partner's ministry to men whose wives had either left them or already divorced them. Based on the stories and information gained I reshaped the book and presented it to the editors at Thomas Nelson, who agreed to publish it—and it is still in print 20 years later.

In 1993 we were temporarily living in Nashua, NH to be close to our son and his family of three little girls when I finished the manuscript for *In the Hands of the Potter.* That morning I talked to the Lord, saying, "Lord, I need either a full-time job or better pay for my book assignments." That afternoon a God Moment occurred when Dr. V. Gilbert Beers, president of Scripture Press, called.

Twenty years earlier Dr. Beers had been in my office at Moody Press with a proposal for six full-color children's books. I brought him into the editorial committee to explain his vision—and Moody Press became his publisher for a dozen or more books. The first set of six was sold door to door in southern states by students during several summers and netted Dr. Beers and Moody rewarding royalties from the distributor's sales.

When Dr. Beers called in May 1993, he began his call with "I'm sitting with Joyce Gibson, the director of our curriculum department, discussing our need for a managing editor. I received your postcard saying you were open to a full-time position. Would you be interested in becoming managing editor of the curriculum division of Scripture Press?" What a God Moment! An interview with key Scripture Press staff at the CBA Booksellers Convention in July resulted in my being accepted for the managing editor position.

**Birth of an Agency**

The interview was, however, only one purpose for attending the booksellers' convention. In another God Moment in spring I had been approached by several writers about becoming their agent. They insisted my background in publishing was important to them as they were looking for a publisher to take on their book projects. After prayer I agreed to represent three writers—and in several months helped each find a publisher. I established a pattern of setting up appointments with editors at the convention and introducing a variety of book proposals to them. At the time publishers were still growing their fiction lines, so a three-novel contract was fairly normal. For the next 11 years I evaluated proposals and sent out selected ones on a part-time basis, focusing on helping first book authors.

Life in the curriculum division at Scripture Press took me back mentally to my years as denominational editor in Canada. For four years I was not only editor of a 12-page weekly publication, but I was also responsible for ordering the Christian bookstore's inventory of English language books. Christian Press for years had operated a second floor bookstore to serve those in German-speaking congregations in Canada. Many of these churches were experiencing the pains of transition to English in Sunday services and needed resources for both Sunday school pupils and teachers. I quickly discovered one of my other responsibilities every quarter became placing curriculum orders for 60 churches with Scripture Press.

Over the years I had also taught high schoolers in Sunday schools using Scripture Press curriculum—and while editorial director at Moody Press I had been free-lancing writing curriculum for junior highs for Urban

Ministries, an offshoot of Scripture Press serving the African American churches. So in a sense I was coming home when I walked into the curriculum division offices at Scripture Press.

## A Technological Revolution

I arrived at Scripture Press in the midst of a technological revolution. Editors each had a Mac on their desk, but we still had to draw on past lesson materials stored in a large computer typesetting database. Five designers had advanced Mac software to develop full color lessons, drawing on illustrations by using storage devices. The completed lesson materials were stored on memory devices and hand carried to the printers. Since I had been working with Microsoft software I had to learn a new computer "language."

With the Mac computers providing new design opportunities, the editorial team developed more modern and full color take-home publications for the middle and senior high curriculum. *Power for Living,* our adult take-home paper, transitioned into full color. We developed new curriculum for adults using devotional material developed by Walk Thru the Bible.

Within six months another God Moment expanded my duties beyond the curriculum department. Dr. Beers called me into his office and offered me the responsibilities of editor of *The Christian Education Journal,* a quarterly publication for directors of Christian Education in churches and professors of Christian Education at colleges and seminaries. This enabled me to attend their annual convention and interact with those able to supply articles. I particularly enjoyed editing articles based on research being done by those in Masters and Ph.D. programs. I gained insights and contacts that aided us when I next served with the Evangelistic Association of New England and helped develop the program for their annual Christian Education Conference.

**Sixty Years of Service**

Celebrating 60 years of service to Christ and the churches became one of the highlights at Scripture Press. Founded by Dr. and Mrs. Victor Corey, Scripture Press featured All Bible Lessons first developed in the 1930s by Dr. Garner, a Christian Education professor at Moody Bible Institute. In time the growing publishing house moved from Chicago to Wheaton, IL, opened a Christian bookstore and eventually began publishing books under the imprint Victor Books. Scripture Press Foundation became the charitable arm. It published the Christian Education Journal, raised money for Bibles and Bible study books for those in prison—and let me employ skills as a writer of fundraising letters.

Not long after the great 60th anniversary celebration we learned that the Board was considering selling the publishing house. We were told the reason was that the megachurch movement was significantly reducing the number of Sunday schools, making the curriculum department a less than profitable division. Two financial analysts disproved that assumption when they finally separated out costs and incomes for both the curriculum department and Victor Books. They uncovered an unpleasant reality—the book program was creating the losses, which the curriculum department's surpluses could not cover. Instead of divesting itself of the money losing department, the administration accepted an offer from David C. Cook Ministries for the whole publishing house.

For the second time I faced an uncertain future as negotiations proceeded toward the sale's consummation. I needed a God Moment. What I did not know was that God had been preparing a new opportunity. One day I opened a newsletter from the Evangelistic Association of New England and out dropped a slip of paper with the news that the Association board had approved the hiring of a Director of Communication and Marketing. I carried the news home and told my wife Rita about it. Her immediate response stunned me: "Apply," she said. My response was, "You'd move again?" And she replied, "In a minute, if I can get close to our granddaughters." I applied, interviewed and we moved from Wheaton, IL to Arlington, MA. We landed in a two-flat within minutes of our son, his wife, and three delightful granddaughters. And to a new series of God Moments.

# 17

## Investing in the New England Church World

If you asked most any pastor or ministry leader in 1996 about the state of Christianity in New England, he or she would parrot a popular perception—the church is dead in New England. When I took over communication and marketing for the Evangelistic Association of New England I knew that was not true, for I had attended the annual gathering of evangelicals in recent years and seen a vibrant community of faith. Over the next five and a half years I had ample opportunity to disprove it in one God Moment after another.

It did not take long for me to recognize the vibrancy and commitment of men and women leading the dozen ministries serving Christ and the church under the umbrella of EANE. Each had to do their own fundraising, but EANE provided a variety of resources to aid them, not the least of them being the mailroom and its computers and photocopiers. As editor for a monthly newsletter going to Christians and churches I saw my job as helping them keep their ministry alive in church leadership circles and budgets. The bi-monthly newsletter to pastors kept them informed on events designed to bring them together and enriched by nationally known speakers.

Two major events required maximum promotion:

- The annual Christian education conference that was held in different regions with a church facility large enough for several hundred Sunday school teachers and leaders, youth ministry leaders, and women's ministry leaders.

- The annual Congress, which brought together eight thousand or more Christians from five states in the Hines Memorial Convention Center in Boston, eager for refreshment and learning new ministry approaches. Evangelism remained a major focus, with scores coming to a personal faith in Christ during the keynote addresses and workshops—and Christians who had never shared their faith introduced to effective personal witnessing.

About six months after we arrived Rita and I experienced a God Moment when we attended the dedication service for the Walnut Hill Community Church's first church building. Organized in our home 15 years earlier, the church had met in school facilities all these years while fighting to erect a sanctuary on property purchased in a community several miles from Danbury. After ten years of litigation their case landed in Connecticut's Supreme Court, which in a God Moment ruled the town had to let them build a church. With a warm-hearted pastor and active members the church started growing exponentially and today the main site has about 2500 in its services, with five church plants.

## Healthy Church Growth Principles Are Born

The Rev. Stephen Macchia, president of the Evangelistic Association, had developed ten principles of a healthy church before I arrived. A team of pastors had interviewed more than a hundred pastors for feedback. My first assignment was to interview pastors all over New England whose church demonstrated one or more of the principles of a healthy church. I was stunned by what I found, discovering growing churches all over New England, often led by can-do pastors from other parts of the United States.

Surprisingly, many of the churches had grown from a hundred or so congregants to 300, 400, even 750 and 900 in worship services. A church in Maine attracted 500 on Sundays when the town had fewer residents than that. A charismatic African American pastor in Boston saw his evangelistically focused church grow to 5,000, with 2,000 in the youth congregation. Another African American pastor in a Hartford, CT suburb had started a church in his home in the 1960s and was building a sanctuary for 7,000 attendees. In a Burlington, Vermont, community, one evangelical church had 750 and another five miles away had 900 at services. We also discovered that pastors that stayed with a church 20 years or more typically led a growing church—and we honored them at a late 1990s Congress of evangelicals. I told their stories in the newsletters to pastors.

At Congress 1998, EANE set up 15 computers and invited attendees to spend 15 minutes ranking the Rev. Stephen Macchia's 10 principles of a growing church on their perceived significance in the growth of a healthy church. With no incentive other than helping in research, 1500 New England believers lined up for their turn to record their rankings. There were numerous surprises, with by far the majority ranking as No. 1 experiencing the presence of God in the services, probably reflecting that Pentecostal and Charismatic churches were frequently the fastest growing. Evangelism and stewardship were down the list from the one on a caring community.

**A Book Is Born**

Now that I had recorded and told the stories of churches reflecting the 10 principles of a healthy church—and we had the research data from the 1500 evangelicals ranking the significance of the principles—we knew it was time for a book. The Rev. Macchia and I storyboarded the sequence of chapters on a chalkboard. He spent the summer writing the book, inserting the already published stories of healthy churches as evidence of where God gave the increase when principles of church health were prayerfully implemented.

As a part-time literary agent I developed a proposal with sample chapters and circulated the proposal to publishers, realizing editors would be skeptical a ministry leader in New England would have the marketing clout needed. An editor at a major publisher expressed interest, but insisted we needed stories gleaned nationally of churches illustrating the ten principles. I told the Rev. Macchia that if a Canadian pastor using only Canadian stories illustrating what it meant to have a vibrant Christian experience could write a bestseller, a book on *Becoming a Healthy Church* featuring only story illustrations from New England ought to sell. Shortly thereafter a Baker Book editor contacted us and expressed interest. We flew to Grand Rapids to meet with the editors and key marketing people and Baker released the book in 1999. That year *Becoming a Healthy Church* sold more than 30,000 copies, more than any Baker non-fiction book released that year. By 2004 it had gone through three printings and it is still available.

## A Bright Idea

One day while employed at what became Vision New England I received a call from Dr. Bill Bright of Campus Crusade for Christ that became another God Moment. Would I be interested in doing the research and first draft of a book on the attributes of God? He had a message he occasionally gave on the topic and was vitally interested in seeing it expanded into a book with his name on it. My research led me to the library at nearby Gordon-Conwell Theological Seminary for several days of research over Thanksgiving. I added book purchases from the used book section of Kregel's bookstore in Grand Rapids, and books on theology from other sources. We followed it up with a meeting with Dr. Bright, his wife Vonette, and several staff, pumping Dr. Bright for stories illustrating the attributes of God as he experienced them. After he personalized the content and an editor inserted the stories, the book became simply *God*.

Then a publisher approached me about a book for a well-known evangelist that had a deadline of two months. This time I could take time off over Christmas and the New Year to do the research and write the book. Completing those two books represented an immersion in Christian doctrine and the Bible's teaching possible only because I had completed four years of Bible college studies years earlier. I had also been involved in many theological discussions leading the Textbook Committee at Moody

Press in the 1970s. As I lead workshops at Christian writers conferences on "Integrating Life Experience with Scripture" in their writing I consistently recommend extended personal biblical and theological studies if a writer is to represent biblical truth accurately.

## A Pending God Moment

Many readers will remember what was called the dotcom bust in the years 2000 and 2001. The stock market meltdown dramatically reduced the income of many charities, including those supporting Vision New England. Everywhere ministries had to cut back—and so did Vision New England. Leadership decided a communications and marketing vice president was expendable, so I was given notice that my services were no longer needed. The resulting God Moment, however, generated a dramatic new opportunity for me as a writer and teacher of writers that I will disclose in the next chapter of *God Moments in My Publishing Life.*

# 18

## Experience Open Doors for God Moments

At Vision New England in Acton, MA staff were intrigued by the "extending your territory" imagery in *The Prayer of Jabez,* a book by Bruce Wilkinson that sold millions more in the first year than any secular non-fiction book ever. We decided to study the book's chapters at lunch. Some of us printed up small posters with Jabez' prayer, "Oh, that you would bless me and enlarge my territory! Let your hand be with me and keep me from harm so that I will be free from pain."

Critics called it a selfish prayer, but so few pastors were challenging their congregants to believe God for achieving beyond initial expectations that it caught fire and small church groups were studying it everywhere. And though already beyond typical retirement age, I put up the poster with the prayer in my office and in faith prayed the prayer daily.

Did God quickly respond? It did not seem that way when I got my notice that I was being released because of budget shortfalls. Then God stepped in with a God Moment. Two weeks before my final day in the office I received an e-mail from Jerry Jenkins announcing he had purchased The Christian Writers Guild from Norm Rohrer. After 37 years of guiding writers in improving their skills, Norm and Virginia were retiring. I responded to Jerry with the news I was being released at Vision New England and was ready to help him in any way. He replied he wanted me on his editorial board.

The real God Moment came after Jerry had me examine the Guild's lessons and I recommended we start over. He called and said, "I am going to announce to the Board that you will be writing a new set of lessons." Astonished, I reminded him I did not have a journalistic degree and he had two retired journalism professors on his board. He replied, "I've followed you through the years and I know you can do it." Talk about God extending my territory in response to me praying the Prayer of Jabez!

I wrote my first correspondence course lesson on writing as a Christian over Labor Day and e-mailed it to Jerry. His over-the-top positive response gave me the courage to continue. Jerry gave me permission to enlist writers for specialized lessons on writing for children (Christine Harder Tangvald), writing poetry (Michael Bugeja), church plays (Paula Bussard), screenplays (Kathy

Mackel), novels (Dave Lambert). I had gotten to know most of those I enlisted at writers' conferences as published writers and workshop leaders. Others Jerry had gained confidence in and had joined the team.

## Tackling the God Assignment

My approach included ordering samples of magazines, take-home papers, and specialized resources that I could use to illustrate publishable writing. The terrorist attack on the World Trade Center on 9/11 resulted in an explosion of colorful, graphic and imagery-rich articles in Boston newspapers that I could draw on as illustrations of great writing for the media. But I knew only the Holy Spirit could give me the insights I needed to resource a generation of writers seeking to improve their skills. Thus every day I opened my computer to an empty screen and prayed, "Holy Spirit, give me the outline for this lesson. Remind me of examples from Scripture and life. Help me shape into usable form the lessons writers need to learn to improve their skills." Even as I was praying God would remind me of an outline, biblical illustrations, life illustrations, sending me to my keyboard. Lessons learned from correspondence courses I had taken, evening school classes, on-the-job journalistic techniques I gained from Robert Walker, founder of Christian Life Publications, as business magazine editor/writer, as freelance writer, newsletter writer, advertising copy writer, and book author came alive as I wrote lessons.

Asking God to extend my territory came alive as I later mentored writers taking the Apprentice and Journeyman Courses, who sent their completed lessons by e-mail from Nigeria, Kenya, Great Britain, South Africa, New Zealand, Canada. He also gave me the opportunity to fulfill a commitment I made in a mine warehouse in northern British Columbia at age 22: to serve the Lord to the maximum of my ability on a worldwide basis.

## Another Surprise Opportunity

God had another surprise in store for me. Stymied in their attempts to enlist a Ph.D. in communication as head of their journalism faculty, Gordon College in Wenham, MA decided to appoint a Journalist in Residence as a stop gap. An associate at Vision New England had moved to Gordon College as director of their media relations and publicity departments and heard of that decision. She recommended me as Journalist in Residence, another God Moment. After several interviews I was invited to join the faculty. Ironically, both our son and his wife were graduates of Gordon College-- and we lived in Haverhill, an easy commute to Gordon College.

I had taught journalism principles in workshops not only in North America but also to Campus Crusade for Christ staff in Europe, the Philippines, and Singapore—and I had just completed 52 lessons in writing journalistically for the Christian Writers Guild. But would my experience-based journalism hold up in an academic environment?

I quickly discovered textbooks previously used did not provide as broad a scope of lesson material as the lessons I had written for Jerry Jenkins. I also enlisted visiting Chapel speakers to join classes and give students an opportunity to practice their interview techniques. I brought in reporters from the daily newspapers to share how their reporting skills were tested during the burgeoning scandal about priests molesting young communicants. I also enlisted Kathy Mackel to lead the first class on screenwriting. And again the Lord extended my territory with four students from Kenya in my classes, one of them a practicing reporter in the capital city

My "extras" during the three semesters I taught included eating lunch in the faculty classroom and listening to conversations unique to academic environments. What a difference from the lunch times with the Moody Bible Institute faculty in 1961, though in both cases political issues connected to an election intruded on weighty spiritual and academic issues!

Getting acquainted with faculty in their lunchroom prepared me for another exhilarating experience— marching in cap and gown with the faculty during the graduation in 2003—it was 52 years since I had worn quite different garb at a graduating ceremony of the Mennonite Brethren Bible College. Two weeks before that graduation ceremony I had agreed to become the founding editor of the *Mennonite Observer*—now I was celebrating graduating Gordon College seniors who had been in my classroom to complete qualifications for their degree. God had brought me full circle.

My next chapter will tackle God Moments as a literary agent. But first I'll introduce a series of God Moments in "everyday life" that brought us to the foothills of the Blue Ridge Mountains in North Carolina in 2004.

# 19

## God's Surprises

The overall title for this series speaks to one of my purposes—to help writers recognize the God Moments in their life. Yet many of the God Moments in my life as a full-time literary agent may not have happened if we had not recognized family-related God Moments.

We started life in Arlington, MA in early 1996 in a second-floor apartment five minutes from our son's home, while hoping to locate a house we could afford. One day our treasurer at Evangelistic Association of New England, in a God Moment, said to me, "We looked at a condo at the Village at Brickett Hill in Haverhill, but it is not quite right for us. You may want to look at it."

I did, then brought my wife Rita to check it out. We decided it suited our purposes, with an office area in the lower level adjacent to a TV viewing area—and a bedroom in the loft on the third floor that could serve as my wife's ironing and sewing room. The large living room could accommodate a good-sized group of people, important for my wife's joy in hospitality. We spent eight happy years there. Just when we thought climbing the stairs between four floors could become a problem with us in retirement age, God set a chain of events in motion that surprised us.

It started when Jerry Jenkins decided Christian Writers Guild ought to sponsor a Christian writers' conference and selected The Cove, the Billy Graham Training Center near Asheville, NC as the site for the first one. Since I was still listed as editorial director and was mentoring apprentices, I was invited to participate. Thinking about it I remembered an editor for a horse book publisher Rita and I had met at a Christian Writers Conference in 1995. She had wanted to write an evangelistic book for horse people and we discussed it at some length.

I knew she had moved to North Carolina and into the horse community of Tryon and was editing a magazine for horse people. An e-mail resulted in an invitation to join them for the weekend previous to the conference. Rex and Maureen gave me a great tour of the town and community in the foothills of the Blue Ridge Mountains--and I discovered the area was also a major retirement community. But it did not seem likely that Rita would be willing to leave Massachusetts, with three granddaughters only 33 miles from us.

God was, however, on the move. Six months later Rita suggested we get a multiple listing book for Polk County, the setting for Tryon. We drove down the day after I turned in the exams I had marked for my journalism students at Gordon College. Guided by a realtor, we saw a number of houses the next morning. Over noon I was paging through a brochure listing houses when I saw one that looked interesting. The description fit what we were looking for—a ranch home with four bedrooms, a larger living room, and a basement. Late afternoon we toured it—and afterward my wife said, "That house met all of my criteria, down to a white galley kitchen." I was overwhelmed by the beauty of what I considered a miniature arboretum around the house and the forested property around it.

On that weekend's Sunday in another God Moment our son called without knowing the reason for our trip, suggested we look around in Tryon as a possible retirement community. Rita heaved a big sigh of relief, since her concern had been his attitude toward us moving. We knew his three daughters were now in their teens and were engrossed in the usual teen activities, so we were not as important to them anymore.

We decided to pray about it for two weeks, reasoning if the Lord wanted us to have the house, he'd save it for us. Convinced after two weeks of extended prayer that God wanted us to move to Tryon, we made an offer, contingent on us selling our condo, and it was accepted. The next day, Memorial Day, we had a realtor at our dining room table discussing a possible sale price for the condo. I was astonished at the price she suggested, mentally calculating if we got it we could pay off our mortgage and pay cash for the Tryon house. We decided on an open house the next weekend, but two days later learned that another buyer had showed up for the Tryon house—and we had to either counter the offer within 72 hours or give it up, since we still had to sell our condo.

God wasn't done yet. A day later our realtor called and said a friend in another town had a client who was looking for a three-bedroom condo in the Village at Brickett Hill. Stunned, I responded, "Don't we have the only three-bedroom condo in the village?" She admitted I was right, so we agreed to let her friend's client visit the next day. In less than 24 hours we had a full-price offer and I could inform the Tryon realtor we could drop the contingency.

In a truly miraculous series of God Moments he had sent us a buyer without our condo being listed—and we had gained a house that was in an incredibly beautiful setting and amazingly fit for what God would do later. The home he got us let us provide extended hospitality to two granddaughters. One of them, Bethany, served as my assistant as she looked for a job after college, which led to her becoming my webmaster while on her new job in the marketing department at Wycliffe Bible Translators in Orlando, FL. God had plans for the house we acquired we could not have dreamed up. All we can do is praise the Lord for all the special God Moments along the way.

My next chapter will focus on the surprises God sent my way as literary agent focused on helping first book authors get published.

---

# 20

---

## Does God Answer Selfish Prayers?

One of the questions most of us have asked is, "Will God answer my selfish prayer?" The answer you have probably received is that he will not. Yet we have an amazing God, whose grace is higher than the heavens, so at times he acts in ways that seem contrary to the rules we have set for God. Let me share some God Moments that exhibit God's grace.

Through eight years at Moody Press I repeatedly experienced God Moments, his grace-filled answers to prayer. Every so often I'd look at the books we had scheduled for the next season and realize we had none with what I called sizzle.

To give our list the attention it deserved I knew we needed to have at least one book that stood out as a sure seller for buyers at bookstores. I'd ask the Lord for two sizzlers that would excite bookstore buyers—and inevitably they would arrive "over the transom." In a God Moment he led me to Dr. Viggo Olsen and his book became *Daktar: Diplomat in Bangladesh,* an instant bestseller. In another one he led me to Zola Levitt, whose *Satan in the Sanctuary* and *The Coming Russian Invasion of Israel,* with Tom McCall, became bestsellers.

Fast forward. I learned to pray a similar prayer as I headed for Christian writers conferences as a literary agent. Some years ago I was asking the Lord for a key author contact as I headed for a Write to Publish Conference in Wheaton, IL During a lunch hour I experienced a God Moment as I set my tray of food on the table opposite a man I had never met. I discovered he was a pastor, who had started a church that had grown to nearly 2,000 attendees. He had written a book for small group leaders that had been published by a curriculum house. We talked about what he would like to write and he confessed that prayer was on his mind.

## The Prayers God Answered

By God's grace Dave Earley signed on as a client. He told me he had been praying the prayers of the Bible and wanted to write on his experience seeing God answer when he prayed those prayers in his life. He came up with *The 21 Most Effective Prayers of the Bible.* I sent out the proposal. Reject after reject arrived. After all, there were many books on prayer and Dave was not yet a household name. A

Barbour editor saw potential and signed up Dave Earley's book idea.

Barbour sent a copy of the book to Choice Books, who put it on their racks as *The 21 Most Effective Prayers of the Bible*. Within six months 60,000 copies had been picked off racks in airports, supermarkets, laundromats, hotel lobbies. Barbour had Dave Earley write book after book for that market. They also repeatedly repackaged the original edition of *The 21 Most Effective Prayers of the Bible*. It was also sold into bookstores and is available on amazon.com.

## A Fast with a Long Life

I distinctly remember praying that I'd find marketable book projects at a conference in Kansas City sponsored by Heart of America Christian Writers Network, not even dreaming I'd find three publishable book projects of real significance.

Kristen Feola presented my biggest surprise. When she told me she was working on a book presenting the Daniel Fast. I asked, "What's a Daniel Fast?" since I had not heard of it. She patiently explained it was a vegetable fast practiced in her large church and in other charismatic churches.

Not yet comprehending the significance of her book project, I asked what would make it stand out. She explained she had set up a mini photo studio in her kitchen to photograph the 100 dishes she was preparing. She also was including the recipes for each dish. She had written three chapters on the Fast and was writing 21 devotionals to go with the 21-day Fast. Now I was intrigued and quickly agreed to represent the book project.

In a God Moment, Kristen's book proposal arrived at Zondervan when they were anxious for a competitor to an existing book by another publisher. They rushed the book to press. Sales of more than 60,000 copies and three successful online January fasts validated the decision to publish *The Ultimate Guide to the Daniel Fast*. Her marketing efforts rewarded her with a successor book, *Spiritually Strong,* which combined Kristen Feola's expertise in physical fitness, nutrition, and spiritual disciplines. An online Bible study in January led by Kristen provided an opportunity to showcase the book.

## A Christian News Reporter's Dream

A former news anchor and at the time a weekend Fox News reporter, Carey Wickersham dreamed of providing a resource for pregnant women that would also benefit the Right to Life proponents. She approached me at the Kansas conference with her dream of a book that would include a meditation, a medical tip, and a photo of a new baby every week of a new pregnancy, taken with amazing 3-D ultrasound images on a new ultrasound equipment operated by a highly skilled technician. She wanted web links and QR codes in the book that would lead to dazzling videos of a baby's growth and new movements every week as it grew.

I did not hesitate. I wanted to represent this dramatic new way of helping future mothers with both information and visual presentations of what happened in a pregnant woman's womb. Publishers did not share our enthusiasm, until it got front and center attention at Focus on the Family Books. With Tyndale House as distributor, Focus on the Family Books got the technical help needed to produce *The Wonder Within,* a stunningly beautiful hardcover book.

## A Discipler's Amazing Tool

As president of Here's Life Publishers I had husbanded into print a one-on-one discipling book by a staff member of Campus Crusade for Christ. It had sold four times as many copies as our marketing people projected, most likely because it had 17 endorsements on the back cover, including some by well-known names.

Kenneth Erisman's book on one-on-one discipling was different. For starters, he had text in various colors. It could be used with new believers or veteran believers who had never studied basic Bible doctrines that could deepen faith. But what stunned me were his endorsers, people like Dr. J. I. Packer, Jerry Bridges, Bruce K. Waltke, Rebecca Pippert, Joni Eareckson Tada, all well-known by Bible students. Where did he get the clout to enlist their support? It had to be what he had written—and it was.

Finding a publisher for *Grounded in the Faith* required patience, since conventional wisdom among marketing people is that evangelism and discipleship books do not sell. After 18 months I had no publishing prospect. Then in a God Moment, Baker Books hired a new editor—and he loved *Grounded in the Faith* and convinced the team to publish it. Sales have been stronger that even I expected.

This reveals a sampling of God responding to what even I would admit were selfish prayers. But God had the long view—he knew there were books being written that would immeasurably bless people. All he had to do was arouse a desire to pray for him to arrange the connections needed.

My next chapter will depart from a citation of God Moments to illustrate how conventional wisdom in publishing can result in serious blunders. Why? Because conventional wisdom looks back instead of forward to God's possibilities.

# 21

## Yes, Publishers Do Blow It

Publishing staff are human and thus susceptible to misjudging opportunities. Let me introduce just some of the most striking examples from Christian publishing that I became aware of as I worked in the publishing industry, including a couple in which I was involved.

My first assignment when I arrived at Moody Press in 1970 was to edit a book by a Canadian presenter of travelogues. The book featured the story of a home missionary, remarkably from my home province, British Columbia, Canada, and my wife's home province, Alberta. It was W. Philip Keller's second venture into writing a biographical Christian book and it needed a lot of work to shape it for publication. So Keller took his second book, *A Shepherd Looks at Psalm 23* to Zondervan. Though Keller had led a lot of Bible studies, he was unknown as a biblical scholar, so the book's sale started slowly. Readers, however, loved it and talked it up, with sales taking off, in time reaching 100,000 copies.

Those sales numbers, however, did not convince Zondervan's editorial and marketing team to take on Keller's next book, *A Layman Looks at the Lord's Prayer.*

"No one is interested in a book on the Lord's prayer," Zondervan editors reported back to Keller. He remembered Moody Press and came to us with the manuscript. The Moody team reasoned Keller had gained enough of a following to risk publishing *A Layman Looks at the Lord's Prayer.* We introduced an edited manuscript to Billy Graham's team, who chose it as its giveaway on his extremely popular "The Hour of Decision." The book the Zondervan team turned down caught on with the listeners to "The Hour of Decision." Several hundred thousand copies ended up in homes all over the U.S., much to the delight of the Moody Press team—and Keller.

## A Different Genre

In the mid-70s a somewhat fictionalized version of Crying Wind's book focusing on Native American life by a practicing Christian arrived at the publishing house where I worked then. Every letter she wrote me as her editor was filled with extremely humorous stories of her children's activities. Editorial staff loved her homey letters featuring a family of five children, several still preschool age. She did not, however, want her name on the cover of the book manuscript so she submitted it as fiction, but marketing insisted it had to be presented as a memoir. The author and I objected, since we knew some of it was fictionalized to protect family members.

The company's marketing department went ahead anyway, giving it the title *Crying Wind,* releasing it as an autobiography—without an appropriate disclaimer on its fictional content. Sales of plus 100,000 copies led to accusations by family members and high school associates that the author had been untruthful. I had moved on to another job when the company's management and the legal department decided to discontinue publishing it—and withheld tens of thousands of dollars of accumulated royalties. During the internal investigation, two simple phone calls to me as former acquisitions editor, or the director of the publishing company would have revealed the reason for the accusations. An emotionally shattered author turned to writing novels for the secular market.

**Misreading the Market**

There are abundant cases of either the whole management team or marketing department misreading the market. At one company, marketing personnel believed that a book with the word "cancer" in the title would not sell. As editorial director I had gained a chapter on cancer in children from the recently retired Surgeon General of the United States, C. Everett Koop, so my boss insisted on the title. Marketing released it in hardcover, meaning its cost increased dramatically. Despite that, and very limited marketing exposure, the book on dealing with cancer sold 40,000 copies in six months, with the marketing director later telling me, "I wish we had supported it with more promotional efforts."

For me, the classic example of misreading the market was a translation of the Pauline Letters by Dr. Kenneth Taylor, Director of Moody Press at the time. His dream was to provide an easy reading version of the Bible, introducing it with the Pauline Letters as *Living Letters*. One day in 1961 the manager of four Moody Bookstores—my boss, and a member of the Editorial Committee—brought me a brown envelope, saying Dr. Taylor wanted me to evaluate the manuscript in it and report on my findings at the next Editorial Committee meeting.

At home I opened the envelope and found a new translation of I Timothy in it. I evaluated it in light of the New Testament original Greek I had studied in Bible college. When I reported my evaluation at the Editorial Committee meeting, I said it was a really quite accurate, popular level translation, though it needed some help with active verbs and punctuation. I then asked who had done the translation. Dr. Taylor bent his head and murmured, "It is not known." I immediately knew it was his and turned red. No action was, however, taken by the Editorial Committee, since Dr. Tayler wanted approval higher up.

Dr. Taylor took the translation project to Dr. Culbertson, then president of Moody Bible Institute, hoping for his approval. Dr. Culbertson gave it a cool reception, commenting on recently published similar efforts. Dr. Taylor then circulated this idea of a personal translation of the Bible, with the *Living Letters* in final editing, to eight Christian publishers. All turned it down. A printer friend did a printing of 2,000 copies of *Living Letters,* which Dr. Taylor marketed to booksellers at a table as they entered the annual Christian Booksellers Convention door—and sold all copies.

A copy found its way to the member of the Billy Graham team who selected books to give away to donors. He decided to offer *Living Letters* to viewers of the "Hour of Decision" TV program. Incredibly, about 500,000 viewers made a donation and received a copy of *Living Letters*, a most remarkable launch of a new book turned down by eight publishers. And it helped Dr. Taylor launch Tyndale House Publishing, which in time became a strong competitor of the publishing houses that had turned down his translation of the Pauline Letters.

## A Publishing Decision that Backfired

Preachers in the middle of the nineteenth century had little use for stories illustrating the key points in their sermon. They might tell an opening joke, but very few had a story illustrating truth being presented. Thus the public was not prepared for a new trend promoted by a homiletics professor, Dr. Haddon Robinson, at Dallas Theological Seminary—and a college preacher not many miles away.

Both emphasized the role of real life stories as illustrations in preaching. One of the "disciples" was the college preacher, Max Lucado, who caught the wave and wrote a Christian living book laced with stories of real people. Tyndale House agreed to publish it. It did not sell well.

When Max Lucado submitted a second manuscript to Tyndale editors, they looked at sales numbers on his first book and said, "No thanks" to his second one. Bad miscalculation. He took the book proposal to Multnomah Press, where John VanDiest, the director, understood the value of what Max Lucado was doing—using stories the way Jesus used parables. Multnomah Press released it under the title, *No Wonder They Called Him the Savior*—and sales exploded, introducing a long-term, multi-book bestselling author to the reading public. Tyndale House never got Max Lucado back as an author, while he wrote a stream of bestsellers for Multnomah Press and later Word Books (later absorbed by Thomas Nelson Publishers).

## Quick Examples

1. Word Books staff worked hard to acquire rights to a book by Dr. Billy Graham, gaining publishing rights for one book after Doubleday had been his publisher for some years. They released the book under the title *Born Again*. To prove they were a savvy, top-level publisher, Word Books printed a reported 800,000 copies on the first print run. They faced a publisher's worst nightmare when more

books were returned unsold by distributors and booksellers than were sold. I was Vice President of Books and Book Clubs at Christian Herald Association at the time and was offered as many as we could use in our book clubs at a closeout price.

2. One well-known publisher gained publishing rights to a Johnny Cash biography. The marketing team decided he was well enough known as a singer/artist to warrant a major promotional outlay leading up to the release of *Johnny Cash*. Rumor in the industry was that they budgeted a marketing outlay designed to sell 500,000 copies of *Johnny Cash*. Instead, industry rumor was that they sold 125,000 copies, leading to the release of key members of the marketing team.

3. Back in the 70s, Dr. Warren Wiersbe suggested Moody Press go after a preacher in Southern California who was speaking on a radio program sponsored by the Lockman Foundation, publisher of the *New American Standard Bible*. As editorial director of Moody Press, I got my boss's approval to approach the Rev. Charles Swindoll, also pastor of a First Evangelical Free Church in Fullerton, Calif. at the time. I received a nice note from the Rev. Swindoll, saying he would let Moody Press have a book by him if Moody Radio Network would air his Bible teaching radio program. My boss passed that response on to the Moody Bible Institute's executives. The opportunity was turned

down and Multnomah Press got the Rev. Swindoll's first books, which quickly became bestsellers.

4. Writers have many stories of being turned down at publishers and then finding success. Five friends of William P. Young decided to come to his aid when his innovative new book, *The Shack,* was turned down right and left. So convinced were they of Young's book's potential they organized a publishing house just for his book. Then they developed a unique marketing program involving the social media, selling directly to book lovers. Reports surfaced that they sold 30,000 copies over the summer. That got the attention of publishing houses—and FaithWords, owned by the Hachette group, acquired the rights and sales reportedly exceeded 10 million copies.

# 22

## The Impact of a Family Faith Heritage

I s there really such a thing as God honoring a family's Christian faith commitment into the third and fourth generation? I'm aware that history reveals some families with a remarkable pattern of Christian faith being passed on from generation to generation. Recent events have forcibly reminded me that I and my family also represent a similar pattern. So to encourage parents, let me tell our story.

One hundred and fifty-five years ago the decision of 18 men in a village in the Ukraine set off a new life movement still reverberating in countries as different as Indonesia, India, Japan, the Congo in Africa, Colombia in South America—in addition to Europe, Canada, and the United States. In that German-speaking community of Mennonites, whose heritage went back through Prussia to The

Netherlands, their Christianity had degenerated into churchianity. A Lutheran minister arrived and brought the message of new life in Christ.

At an 1860 meeting of the church 18 men, including my great-grandfather, Peter Stobbe, objected to communion being served to members whose behavior revealed little desire to live a godly life. They were summarily dismissed—and the Mennonite Brethren Church was born, marked by aggressive evangelism. Their insistence that people be born again Christians, with a lifestyle to match that of Jesus, before being given communion, so offended the larger community that social ostracism and persecution erupted.

One of the leaders of this new church headed for St. Petersburg, then Russia's capital city, and over two years of effort gained a land grant in the Caucasian Mountain's foothills. Along with about 400 my great-grandfather moved his family there. God used the constant witnessing of the believers in this new church movement to eventually bring one-third of Ukraine's Mennonites into a personal faith in Christ.

## From Russia to Canada

In 1911 my grandfather, John P. Stobbe, son of Peter Stobbe, and a Christian and Bible student, left Russia and brought his family to Saskatchewan, Canada. They eventually moved to British Columbia, but not before the oldest son, my father, Peter J. Stobbe, had traveled to

Hillsboro, Kansas to enter Tabor Academy as a 23-year-old student.

At Tabor Academy my father met my mother, Marie Harder, born in Nebraska of another mission-minded Mennonite Brethren family, who had migrated there from the Ukraine in the early 1870s. Two of my mother's sisters had married foreign mission minded men, who took them to China for years of evangelism and church building there. One of Mom's nephews, Roland Wiens, also became a missionary to China, then to Japan, when the newest Maoist rulers took over China.

My father brought my mother from Kansas to British Columbia to join his parent's growing family, though they made a stop in Los Angeles for one semester of study at the Bible Institute of Los Angeles. I was born soon after they joined my grandparent's family—as did an increasing number of Stobbe cousins. When the growing Stobbe families moved to Abbotsford, B.C, they settled on four farm acreages within a half mile of the U.S. border.

## The Faith Emphasis Expands

That's when my parents, the Peter J. Stobbe's, nurture of us five children was enhanced by the Stobbe "clan" gatherings at my grandparents. Every anniversary and holiday filled the house with adults and children. Conversation often focused on the new church we had helped build, with several uncles in leadership positions. Singing of hymns, accompanied by musical instruments, filled the air. By the time I was nine I was attending Bible studies on the Letters of Paul at my grandparent's house. As a teen I began teaching in a mission Sunday school, participating in evangelistic street meetings, going door to door with tract distribution and personal visits. One of my uncles took me to un-evangelized communities to teach in Vacation Bible Schools. As I entered a local Bible Institute my uncle Abe Stobbe would take me along to a church plant to preach at the evening service.

Other Stobbe uncles and aunts modeled mission commitment. One family became missionaries to First Nation Canadians in western Canada, two uncles and aunts moved to northern British Columbia to plant a church for miners, loggers, and reach out to the First Nation Canadians. A cousin and another uncle spent time in mission work in Asia. I joined the two families in northern British Columbia one summer, working in a mine, participating in church activities and street meetings.

One week at the mine I read Scripture and prayed about my future. I made my commitment to serve my Lord to the maximum of my ability on a worldwide basis. He has honored that commitment. Laid aside on a hospital bed from a mountain climbing injury, I ordered the seven-lesson "The Beginning Christian Writer," which laid the foundation for a 65-plus-year career in article writing, magazine editing, mission promotional writing, curriculum writing, book editing, book writing and publishing,

That commitment to Christ spilled over to cousins, one of whom became a pastor, while some became foreign missionaries. When we had a Stobbe family reunion it was like an extended church service, with lots of music and sharing of what God was doing.

## Mission Commitment Reinforced

My educational trajectory took me to the Mennonite Brethren Bible College in Winnipeg in 1953. At Christmas of my senior year I joined students from our college and two universities to travel to Intervarsity's Urbana, IL missionary conference. There God moved me to interview with Kenneth Taylor of Moody Press, not dreaming that six years later he would invite me to become the floor supervisor of the Moody Bookstore. Upon graduation in 1955 God gave me the assignment to initiate a new denominational weekly publication, aggressively covering the M.B. Church's foreign mission outreach.

At that point God brought my wife, formerly Rita Langemann, into my life when she entered the music program at the M.B. Bible College. She also came from a Christian home and had been involved in musical mission outreach. A year after our marriage it was our turn to start carrying forward the faith legacy we had received.

As we moved because of new job opportunities we always got deeply involved in a Bible-centered and mission-minded church. In fact, in 1981 we were asked to lead in the formation of a new church in our town, Danbury, CT. What started as six couples became 125 in the first Sunday morning service—and is now Walnut Hill Community

Church, with 2500 in weekend services and at least five church plants.

In 1977 we helped our daughter Carol attend that year's Urbana Missionary Conference—and it changed her career goals from music to nursing. Carol and Dale's daughter Becca and our son's daughter, Charlotte, graduated from Biola University, the successor to what my father had attended in 1929.

Our son Gerry attended the 1980 Urbana Missionary Convention, and as a result spent a summer doing mission outreach in Austria. As family they participated in multiple mission trips to the Caribbean. Most amazing, their daughter Bethany, our oldest granddaughter, is now working in the marketing department at Wycliffe Bible Translators—after she attended the Urbana Missionary Conference in 2012 as a college student. She had studied one semester in London and one in Tanzania, Africa—great preparation for working at Wycliffe.

God said unto the fourth generation—and in the Stobbe family the fifth generation is now living out their faith commitment. We have a faithful God!

# 23

## Reflections at Age 90

I was asked to write reflections as my 90th birthday approached. Earlier reflections on *God Moments in My Publishing Life* were intended to capture experiences in the publishing world. They did not reflect family background, married life, church life, and community involvements, including a lifelong interest in sports writers' personality stories.

Through all my life runs a deep awareness of God, his Word, and his movements in my life. It started with my parent's daily family devotions and prayer, at first in the German language and switching to English when we five children gradually entered public school. After scarlet fever at age five my eyes had crossed and for seven years I was odd-man-out in all sports and social activities. I became a voracious reader of books, both Christian and secular.

153

At the same time my life preparation continued in the South Abbotsford Mennonite Brethren Church, where at age six I participated in the church's Christmas event, devoted to public participation by all children. By age 16 I was my Sunday school teacher's assistant and at 18 a neighbor and I taught a preteen boys class both in church and a mission outreach Sunday afternoon. In my mid-teens my neighborhood friend and I also signed out books for others in the church library, while devouring every missionary biography and apologetic book.

All of these experiences coalesced into who I became as a writer and editor because God had a plan for my life. It surpassed anything anyone in my acquaintance circle could have imagined as they bullied me and made fun of my crossed eyes.

## Life-Altering God Moments

I was the oldest in a family of five children, three boys and two girls. In my early teens I was Mom's laundry and garden assistant. After four years in a nearby elementary school I was getting up at 6:00 a.m. to feed and milk cows, then walk half a mile to catch the school bus. After school we helped clear land, plant and hoe silage corn, tend acres of raspberries and strawberries, help mother take care of a large garden and with canning and drying of vegetables and fruit.

Berry picking started in late May, as did potato harvesting. Haying season started in June and included collecting hay from several sources, loading it into our barn's hayloft. By age 16 I was 6'3" and 190 pounds, so I was expected to "do a man's job," especially since Dad had asthma and was allergic to a lot of what we had to process on the farm.

My parent's decision to enroll me in the newly organized Mennonite Educational Institute not only gave me an education in English literature, science, agriculture, but it also included a daily immersion in biblical studies and memorization. I followed that up by completing a four-year Bible Institute program in t wo years, What really paid off later were the classes in preaching, in duties connected with being a pastor. I also learned more about leading music in a church community.

A year at the University of British Columbia introduced me to the diversity of Christian experience as I participated in Intervarsity Christian Fellowship studies led by an Anglican priest. A guest speaker, Dr. Smith, introduced me to the power of story as he retold the story of the man born blind, as told in chapter nine of the Book of John. I also discovered a new version of apologetics in C.S. Lewis's writings.

In 1952 I joined three other young men on an adventurous trip to my uncle and aunt's mission outreach in northern British Columbia, ostensibly to work at a silver, lead, and zinc mine. When I was asked to replace the first aid and warehouse-man, I moved in with miners who appreciated my care after injury. I had lots of evening free time and I dedicated one week to prayer and Bible study in search of what God might have in mind for me in terms of vocation. God convinced me through prayer and Scripture reading that if I dedicated my future to him on a worldwide basis he would provide the plan.

Several weeks later a mountain climbing accident forced a four-month hospital experience. Lying flat on my back I was paging through a Christian magazine. I saw an advertisement shouting "You Can Write." I realized I could afford the $15 required for a 7-lesson correspondence course, "The Beginning Christian Writer." I was hooked.

In 1953 I spent six months in a B.C. Forest Ranger's office, reporting weather and drawing land maps. But I also read most of C.S. Lewis's books, books on Christian psychology, and studied the book of Romans. And I increased my typing speed.—a huge benefit when I became an editor. I visited the services of each church on the island, stood in for a pastor on vacation, leading services both Sunday morning and First Nation's amazing evening testimony/sing-alongs.

## Career and Marriage Decisions

When I headed for two years at a Bible college that fall I still had no idea what God really had in mind for me, but I became a writer. I covered speakers and wrote articles summarizing their message. The college president noticed and made me the college's PR person. Incredibly, I still had no inkling of God's future for me until one spring day I was selling college yearbooks when I landed at a German language weekly publisher's house. In a true "God Moment" I was invited onto his porch. He shocked me by saying he was planning to invest in an English equivalent of his German Mennonite weekly. He asked if I would be willing to be the founding editor. Three months later we released the first edition.

I was now 25 and wondering who God would introduce as a life partner. That fall Rita Langemann, who I had heard sing beautifully at a denominational conference, enrolled in Mennonite Brethren Bible College, where I had graduated in spring. My office was a couple of blocks from my alma mater, so I wandered over at lunch for volleyball, Sunday evenings for their social hour—and saw Rita in action. A friend from her home community encouraged me to approach her. I took the hint. God put us together in a ministry situation and I liked what I heard from her. We were engaged graduation evening and married early September 1956.

A year later a daughter, Carol, arrived and our son Gerry was added to our family in 1960. My commitment to God's purposes took us from Winnipeg, Canada, to British Columbia, then to Chicago and several cities in the U.S. where God was able to use me not only in the publishing world but also in pulpit supply and church leadership positions.

Over 65 years ago I knew God not only had a plan for my life, but also for my musically gifted wife. Determined to fulfill my role as husband, I would initiate contacts she needed until in time she gained the courage to move into opportunities on her own. Her ministry as soprano soloist in "Messiah" performances, in radio drama, as choir leader, music teacher in an elementary school, and community opera, always reflected her deep commitment to God's purposes beyond being a mother and wife.

Today our extended family features a diversity of talents but still an underlying commitment to the Stobbe heritage of Christian service. Our son Gerry's three daughters reflect that as Bethany, married to a teacher, Bud Vander Kaay, manages communications at Wycliffe Bible Translators; Lillie as nurse married to Dr. Ben Luce; Charlotte in promotion and married to GianCarlo Greco, an architectural graduate. Carol and Dale O'Neil's family: son Max, working as asset auditor at Lockheed Martin, and married to Michele, a nurse, and daughter Becca, a teacher, married to Eric Kronibusch, who works in the medical equipment field.

# 24

## The Impact of Book Movements on Publishing

What did it take to launch movements in Christian publishing?

Was it a visionary like D.L. Moody in the late 1800s insisting his Bible Institute students take home five books to sell after founding the Bible Institute Colportage Library? In 1941 the Colportage Library morphed into Moody Press, but only after moving 12 million inexpensive paperbacks into homes all over America.

Was it a publisher like Kenneth Taylor, frustrated with his difficulty in understanding the King James Bible, spending more than a decade doing his own translation/

adaptation that became *The Living Bible*? It sparked a Bible translation movement that still continues.

Or was it Janette Oke, the wife of a Bible college president in Didsbury, Alberta, Canada writing a series of prairie romances simple enough for a 12-year-old and a barely literate grandma to enjoy?

Finally, might it have been fiction writer Jerry Jenkins teaming up with theologian Tim LaHaye to write 16 bestselling futuristic novels based on a prophetic series of events presented in the Bible? Jerry and Tim's series sparked an extraordinary interest in prophetic books.

## The Colporteur Movement

Bible colporteurs were a fixture in the late 1800s, going door to door to combine selling books with an evangelistic fervor. In 1895 D.L. Moody's Bible Institute Colportage Association published *All of Grace,* by C.H. Spurgeon, a world-famous British preacher to thousands in London, England. It sold for 20 cents. The most popular fiction book was *Rosa's Quest,* which sold for decades. Fifteen full-time Colporteurs sold Bibles and the Colportage's books at that point.

That Colportage movement also resulted in the distribution of 15-volume mini-libraries to schools throughout the Appalachian states from 1921 until the end of the century. No wonder that as thousands of school children every year read Christian books, the region became the most Christian in America.

## New Translations Expand Bible Reading Movement

Pictures in media in the early '70s showed hillsides populated by young people in the Jesus Movement reading the Bible—and not just any Bible, but the just published *Living Bible*. I gloried in the sight, since I had been actively involved in getting the first segment, *The Living Letters* edited. I was there when in 1962 Dr. Kenneth Taylor stood behind a table just outside the entrance to the annual Christian Booksellers Convention to sell *The Living Letters* to Christian Booksellers. He sold out the first printing of 2,000, printed on credit by a printer friend.

The booksellers' selling job was made vastly easier when the Billy Graham people chose *The Living Letters* as a giveaway on Graham's national radio program. The *Living Letters* exploded nationally when around 500,000 listeners wrote in for a copy—with a donation for Graham's radio outreach. It demonstrated the impact of national media exposure on a new book. When the completed *The Living Bible* was introduced in 1971 it became the bestselling book in the United States in the years 1972-74, according to *Publishers Weekly*.

Parallel to the years of intensive translation focus by Kenneth Taylor was his development of Tyndale House Publishers, launched in 1962 to introduce the first segment of what became *The Living Bible*. That coincided with me becoming the editor of *Christian Bookseller Magazine,* creating another opportunity for me to promote the new Bible sensation to Christian booksellers.

By the late 1960s the *Good News Bible*, the brainchild of Eugene Nida, head of translation activity at American Bible Society, provided a more readable alternative to the King James Bible. Initially it was seen as a competitor to *The Living Bible,* but it soon became clear it had a different readership.

In 1978 Biblica (International Bible Society) released the *New International Version* (NIV) translation. Zondervan Publishing gained marketing rights to this more exacting, yet still popular level translation of the original Hebrew and Greek sections of the Bible. Originated by scholars in 1956, the NIV has been revised several times as pastors began using it. It became more popular than the *King James Bible*, *the American Standard Bible,* an accurate modernization of the *King James Bible,* or the *New King James* Version, which the president of Thomas Nelson Publishers, Sam Moore's competitive spirit engaged scholars to compete with the New International Version (NIV). Despite the new competition, *The Living Bible*, aggressively marketed not only into the Christian bookstore world but which was also creatively positioned for sales into the general market, kept market share.

This availability of numerous translations of the Bible, enhanced by the accompanying study Bibles, provided new streams of steady income for publishers and bookstores into the 1980s and beyond.

Even though most U.S. homes have a Bible, a Fox News reporter in early April 2020, found that the Coronavirus pandemic resulted in a dramatic increase in Bible sales. One publisher of books of the Bible had a 134 percent increase in sales over the previous year. Other publishers also reported significant increases, with Tyndale reporting a 62 percent increase in Bible sales. Adding to the focus on the Bible was a Fox News special series headlined "America Together: Bible Study Messages of Hope."

## Fiction Comes Alive in Christian Publishing

While not a fiction reader during World War II, I volunteered at our church library's desk as a 15-year-old, helping to check out books. I took home biographies of the great missionaries of the Christian churches. The fiction writers whose names I remember, Grace Livingston Hill and Sallie Lee Bell, were that era's top sellers. Ten years later they still had little real competition. One Canadian author initiated a dramatic revival in fiction.

Janet Oke's first prairie romance, *Love Comes Softly,* selected as a potential winner by Carol Johnson, wife of the president of Bethany House in Minneapolis, exploded on the market in 1979. Rumors set its sales at 400,000 copies— and with that the book launched a surprising new fiction movement. Seventy-five books later movies and television specials added to the significance of her novels and made fiction acceptable reading for Christian women, even teenagers.

While many more sophisticated readers considered Janet Oke's plots too simplistic, a new generation of Christian fiction writers provided novels that satisfied that generation. As the 20th century arrived a generation of writers exploited the publics' new interest in the simplicity of Amish culture—and a new fiction movement was born. Even general market houses acquired fiction authors who specialized in Amish-centered novels.

## Women Authors Cross Boundaries

For decades two factors kept Christian women in their place. One was lack of advanced education and the other was the determination by Christian leaders to keep women "in their place." Every few years an educated woman would break through with a book that gained many readers, usually released by a general market publisher, and rarely did they write more than one book. As we advanced into the second half of the last century both factors began to change. Consistent agitation by women in the larger denominations created opportunity, though the topics they wrote about were few.

Authors like Elizabeth George, Nancy DeMoss Wolgemuth, Beth Moore, Sheila Walsh might be considered the first wave generating interest in books by women who had learned the art of public speaking at training sessions.

Stormie Omartian wrote a series of top-selling books on prayer. The founder of the Proverbs 13 movement, Lysa Terkeurst, burst onto the national scene with deeply thoughtful books on practical Christian living. Ann Voskamp, a Canadian, vaulted to the top rungs of the bestselling list with *One Thousand Gifts*.

A missionary to Australia, Sarah Young, wrote a daily diary that became a daily devotional book, *Jesus Calling*. Initially published by a small new publisher. sales were slow. When Thomas Nelson acquired the publisher, it became the property of the gift books editor. Her enthusiasm for it communicated to the marketing team and sales took off, generating sales of at least 10 million—and a sequel and a series of ancillary products.

**Women in Fiction**

The expansion of the adult fiction market created other opportunities for women writers. But Jan Karon's experience illustrates the difficulties in getting acceptance. Her first book was published by a small publisher in England, even though her setting was Boiling Springs, North Carolina, a mountain town in western North Carolina. A Raleigh, NC. bookseller fell in love with the novel and urged a sales rep from a New York publisher to introduce it to her editors. They agreed to publish it as *At Home in Mitford*, but the *New York Times* fiction reviewers turned up their noses at it and refused to review it. A series of Mitford novels followed, making her a bestselling author.

Francine Rivers was a top-selling author in the general market. She stopped writing novels after a deeply personal experience of the salvation offered by Jesus Christ. She delved into what her experience meant and how it should be reflected in fiction. After four years she wrote *Redeeming Love* as an expression of her faith. It became a bestseller and was followed by a series of novels, all bestsellers.

The explosion of interest in Amish novels created more opportunities for women novelists. Meanwhile the birth of the American Christian Fiction Writers (ACFW) annual conventions generated extraordinary opportunities for personal growth and new contacts for fiction writers.

## The Storytelling Radio Preachers Arrive

Preparing sermons for 52 to 100 occasions a year results in a lot of repetition. So Charles Haddon Spurgeon enlivened his world famous sermons with illustrations, stories—and they were reprinted in daily newspapers all over the world toward the end of the 1800s. For decades few American preachers, especially in evangelical churches, followed his example. As editorial director at Moody Press, I presented to the editorial department in the 1970s a book by a pastor who loved using stories. Marketing staff scorned the storytelling preacher's material even while storytelling preachers were being trained in an evangelical seminary.

Dr. Haddon Robinson, Professor of Homiletics at Dallas Theological Seminary and a master at using stories in his preaching, introduced his students to the role of story in Jesus' teaching. Three graduates of the 1960s took that admonition to heart and are still on national radio as pastors—and each is a prolific author whose books consistently show up on bestseller lists.

In 1980 Dr. Charles Swindoll's *Improving Your Serve,* loaded with great anecdotes, personal stories, reached number one on the Christian publishing bestseller list. It beat out a well-known financial expert's book prophesying a coming economic disaster. One bestseller after another by Charles Swindoll followed. Then another storytelling pastor, Max Lucado, hit the publishing jackpot with one top-selling book after another. At one point his name appeared on the six top sellers in Christian publishing.

The movement expanded as Jesus' use of stories as illustration infected more pastors. When the megachurch in the television era was born and exploded on the American scene, story-oriented preaching increased.

## A Prophecy Movement Expands Book Sales

In 1970 a new Zondervan book, Hal Lindsey's *The Late Great Planet Earth,* which promised to guide Christians into a new era of Christ's reign on earth, grabbed young and old's attention. Launched with little fanfare, its intriguing title titillated readers with explosive predictions of events leading up to Christ's return. Its sales dominated the market in the 1970s, eventually selling more than seven million copies. Recognized as an unimaginable quantity for a prophetic book title, that level of sales spawned a series of look-alikes at other publishers. Some also quickly exceeded normal sales expectations and solidified the financial foundation of several publishers.

The interest in prophecy, and the battle between God and Satan for control on earth, received a new jolt when Crossway Books released Frank Peretti's *This Present Darkness,* rejected by a reported 15 publishers. Three years later this author's *Piercing the Darkness* again grabbed the interest of young people, who implored their parents to read the book. A youth pastor, Peretti's speaking ability further expanded sales, so over the next few years 15 million copies of his books sold through the usual bookstore channels.

## Breaking into the General Market

Despite the successes, Christian books, with the exception of Bibles, still had not gained a real foothold in the general bookstore market in the early 1990s. The dam broke with Tim LaHaye's and Jerry B. Jenkins' first book, *Left Behind,* published by Tyndale House in 1995. Two factors forced ABA bookstores to begin stocking the *Left Behind* series—a cover story in *Time Magazine* that included a review of the book, and a review in The *New York Times,* the first such review of an obviously Christian book by an evangelical publisher. Aiding the distribution into the general market was Tyndale's penetration of it with *The Living Bible,* creating a distribution pathway with smart marketing techniques. With the general market opened, the Left Behind sales exploded, with more than 63 million copies sold of the 16 books in the series. Even today 15,000 copies of the Left Behind series are sold every month.

In the 1992 Moody Press released a book by a marriage speaker who had been promoted by Moody Bible Institute on a speaking circuit. Released as *The Five Love Languages, How to Express Heartfelt Commitment to Your Mate*, it quickly joined other books on the topic. Nearly 30 years later it continues to reveal extraordinary staying power on the general market, consistently showing up on the top 10 of the *New York Times* bestseller list, with millions sold.

This snapshot of movements in Christian publishing is personal. I experienced 65 years of it in most of their manifestations, closely monitoring it as I moved from selling books to ghost-writing books, to publishing books and to agenting author's books. And as a writer coach I am still receiving publishing news every week.

# 25

## Overcoming Challenges Writers Face

I had been asked to speak on overcoming challenges. I decided to focus on overcoming challenges as a writer. Let me not preach at you but hopefully regale you with stories illustrating overcoming challenges as a writer. As you read this chapter I hope you will be thinking, "Wait a minute. Now I know why God let me have that experience." Or you may be thinking, "Whoa, I know now how I can better prepare for overcoming writing challenges."

God does have strange ways at times to prepare us for a challenge as writer. I was 25 and single, weeks away from graduating from Bible college, and writing my testimony for a chapel presentation. Yet what do you say when you are 25 and still don't know what God has in mind for you? Two weeks before the end of the school year I was walking the streets of Winnipeg, Canada, on a sunny May Day selling, of all things, our college yearbook, determined to win first prize in the annual sales contest. I landed at the home of the publisher of a German Mennonite weekly, who was sitting on his porch and said, "Come sit down." After I sat down the publisher said, "At the next meeting of our board two months from now I will be asking the board to approve the founding of an English equivalent of our German weekly. Would you like to be the editor?"

So what had I done to prepare to overcome the challenge of developing a weekly for a denomination that had not had an English publication? God led me to prepare for writing weekly editorials and articles in his unique way.

1. While working as first aid and warehouseman at a silver and zinc mine after my sophomore year in university, I spent a week before the Lord asking what he wanted from me. He made it clear that he wanted me to be a messenger for him, but when or how I had no clue. In prayer I committed myself to have as great an impact as possible on a worldwide basis. A few weeks later a mountain climbing accident put me in the local mission hospital. While flat on my back for three and a half months I saw an ad that shouted, "You can write." I enrolled in The Beginning Christian Writer course, seven lessons for $15. I did my lessons the next summer on an island while employed by the B.C. Forest Service. The weekly editor on that island had all the lessons from the journalism course of the Newspaper Institute of America—and he lent them to me.

2. That fall I arrived at the Bible college, having studied and written all summer. Before the classes started I walked down the street to the denominational publishing house and approached the publisher, asking if he had any proofreading opportunities. Turned out he did. Though he soon discontinued the publication, he had seen my work.

3. I began writing articles based on interviews for a weekly Mennonite publication. Christmas of my senior year the president of the college asked if I would tackle doing publicity for the college. I agreed—and among others submitted articles to the publisher for whom I had done proofreading. That publisher was the one who invited me to become founding editor of his new weekly.

What can we glean from my experience?

1. We can overcome challenges only if we are in touch with the Lord and moving forward in the opportunities he presents. I would never have entered the journalistic field without doing the assignments in that seven-lesson course on writing news articles. Ironically, nearly 50 years later Jerry Jenkins asked me to write the lessons for a new Apprentice Course.

2. The Lord gives us all kinds of life experiences and challenges that prepare us for a future challenge. For two years, 1960-62, I was manager of the selling floor of the Moody Bookstore at Moody Bible Institute. Every week we had groups of African

American kids wandering into the store. Little did I know that 10 years later I would be challenged to write Junior High Sunday school curriculum for African American inner-city kids. Those kids flooding the store helped me visualize who I was writing for. What job has been preparing you for a writing challenge? You may not be seeing it now, but faithful service leads to the Lord giving you a new challenge.

3. Sometimes what we volunteer for is part of God's preparation for a writing challenge. While working almost round the clock as founding editor of the British Columbia Business Journal in the late 1960s, I volunteered to work with the Christian Service Brigade kids in our church because our son was in the 8-11-year-old group. Every week I worked with those kids on their projects, told them stories, listened to their conversation. God saw that as preparation for a new challenge.

In 1970 we had moved to Glen Ellyn, IL for my new job as editorial director at Moody Press. One day the editorial director at the head office of Christian Service Brigade jumped over our back fence and knocked on our door. His mission? "The writer for the Bible study in our magazines is chronically late—and this time I am up against the deadline and no Bible study," he told me. Would I be willing to write a Bible study?

Well, our son was again involved in Christian

Service Brigade, so sure. I delivered a creative new approach to Bible study involving a fiction story based on our son's experiences the next evening. I wrote that Bible study for 10 years. My two years as volunteer interacting with boys had prepared me! Ten years later we put 12 of those Bible studies into book form and the Billy Graham Evangelistic Association picked it up and sent it to kids who accepted Christ at Crusades.

Your focus may be on writing a novel or a non-fiction book, but what volunteer opportunity does God have waiting for you that will help you overcome a writing challenge?

Sometimes one challenge is God's preparation for an even more difficult challenge. When the apostle Paul arrived in Jerusalem after his fourth missionary journey he was rushed by a mob of misinformed zealots. They had heard he was actively witnessing to Gentiles and even bringing them into the temple in Jerusalem. He was rescued from the mob by Roman soldiers, who later under cover of darkness escorted him out of Jerusalem to Caesarea, where he lay in prison for two years. He was brought out of prison to testify before both the Roman governor and the King Agrippa, whom the Romans had appointed king over the whole region. He met those two challenges with presentations so brilliant that the Roman governor exclaimed, "Your learning has made you mad."

Yet God was using these opportunities to testify before secular rulers to prepare Paul for an even greater challenge, an appearance before the Roman emperor. But God had still more challenges to prepare him for that—travel through the greatest storm the Mediterranean could throw at the ship carrying the apostle Paul and his Roman captors to Rome. His challenge was to keep up the spirits of the ship's crew and captain during about three weeks of continuous storm. And God helped him do that by appearing to him at night and encouraging him.

While I had written or ghosted 14 books and hundreds of articles, written scores of newsletters and fundraising letters for Christian organizations, and done public relations for others, I faced my greatest writing challenge in September 2001. Jerry Jenkins had announced to his new board for the Christian Writers Guild that Les Stobbe would be writing a new apprentice course in writing and inviting others to write specialty lessons. I had no degree in journalism, no experience as a professor of journalism or writing, though I had taught English in high school and journalism workshops at writers' conferences for decades.

But when I sat down at my keyboard and faced a blank screen I was faced with a huge challenge. So every day for three months I bowed my head before the computer screen and asked the Holy Spirit to give me the outline and the points I needed to cover for Lesson 1, then Lesson 2, then Lesson 3, and so on for 34 lessons. In a truly unbelievable, amazing way the Holy Spirit gave me the opening ideas, the outline for each lesson. I am a living illustration of the apostle Paul's statement in Philippians 4:13 that "I can do all things through Christ that strengthens me."

What challenge are you facing? Know that God has been aware of it throughout all eternity and has been preparing you through one challenge after another for the one you are facing right now.

# 26

## Communicating Heavenly Ideas in Earthly Terms

As dawn breaks over a Midwest city in a thriving agricultural valley the sun's first rays reflect off the stained-glass windows of a large Roman Catholic cathedral. The streets surrounding it are alive with worshipers, the unsteady gait of the elderly pedestrian. A city bus belching fumes pulls away after disgorging a stream of early morning worshippers, while automobiles edge their way through the approaching worshippers into the parking lot.

What attracts these worshippers to early Mass? Is it merely habit? Or is there something about Catholic worship that appeals Sunday after Sunday to people who by nature like to slip into church on the day they do not need to work—in addition to their workday worship.

In contrast, across town all is still silent at the large Bible church. Its members are not even yawning and stretching yet. In fact, the only movement in the area is the lonely paper boy plopping the Sunday's half-pound of newsprint in driveways.

When the Bible church faithful gather at 11 a.m., the lobby is crowded with in-transit latecomers who rush in to find a seat during the choral introit or the pastoral prayer. Instead of kneeling in prayer for a moment of worship, as do their Catholic friends across town, they reach out and shake the hand of a friend who has his eyes half open during the pastoral prayer. The sun joins the congregation through clear glass windows, with no symbolic statement interrupting its path.

Why did the Catholic worshippers go to church? I suspect they probably went to experience a sense of the transcendent, to absorb the greatness of God as depicted in symbol. They go home feeling they have somehow been in the presence of God.

Why do the Bible church member attend church? I'm convinced they go to hear truth proclaimed, to express the great truths of Scripture in song, and to gain new insights into how God works in the world today. Sermons tend to be expository statements that are heavy on teaching content. As the Bible church members leaves the church they may say, "Good sermon, Pastor," and ride off feeling vaguely guilty for not being a better Christian. Rarely do they get the kind of specific application needed to begin witnessing to a neighbor, reaching out in love to a neighbor ill in the hospital, or discipling his teen son more effectively. All too rarely will some say as they drive off with their family, "You know, I really met God in the worship service this morning."

When I interviewed Dr. Helmuth Thielicke, the Hamburg theologian and pastor whose books influenced a whole generation of U.S. pastors in the 1950's and '60's, about great preaching, I also asked him about the role of liturgy. He said, "The strength of liturgy is that in it we preserved the essential message of the Gospel through all the hundreds of years of the dark ages. The services always contained the essential core of the Gospel, so that it could blossom forth during the Reformation."

As a then longtime member of a church with no liturgy, I found that an intriguing statement. And it came back to me with renewed force when I read a statement by the writer Sallie TeSelle that there can be no statement of transcendent reality which is not metaphorical. In other words, it does not have some sort of symbolic content. And I thought about the Psalmist writing, "O Lord, our Lord, how majestic is your name in all the earth. You have set your glory above the heavens" (Psalm 8:1 KJV).

Stop for a moment and list some of the words people use for God: righteous, holy, majestic, love, all-powerful, all-knowing. Do they begin to plumb the depths of how we actually experience God? If an aborigine from Australia who has never heard about the God of the Bible walked in, would these words describe God to him?

How does the Psalmist describe God? Look at Psalm 19:1-6 for the way he introduces God. Only after he has established the overwhelming greatness of God by the use of metaphor and simile does he begin his straightforward statements about the law of God. Or consider Psalm 91, where the nature of God and his care for us is expressed through metaphor and comparison.

What does a metaphor do that a simple, straightforward statement cannot accomplish? A simple statement tends to work at only one level, while a metaphor works at two levels.

Consider the statement: "His love is gentle."

Now let's turn it into a simile: "His love is like dew settling as the dawn breaks across the sky."

If I break down each sentence, the words are all the ordinary, garden variety. Yet the second sentence carries an image of something elusive. These words are a reflection of something of which they are now a symbol. In this secondary, poetic sense, they point to a reality which transcends the everyday meaning of the word.

Consider another situation. My wife and I loved to go to the zoo. When we moved to California we visited the San Diego zoo several times. As we walked through it we saw all those animals from the wilds of Africa, Asia, and Eurasia. As you read those words you may have a mental image of tall pampas grass, of gnarled tropical trees, of lush forests, and of gazelles running across a plain at 60 miles an hour.

Yet remember, I was in the San Diego zoo. So I have to report that the animals are behind bars, that they live in cages. Immediately a whole galaxy of emotions are released because bars and cages speak of captivity, and no one likes captivity. The bars are not just lengths of iron welded together by my friend, Grady, the steel fabricator. They are also a symbol of loss of freedom.

The reality is that each of us learns our words in the tangible world of lengths of steel bars. When a baby first says "Da, da," it probably is facing reality in the person of the father. In my case, it was 6'3" and 210 pounds when our son, Gerry, first mouthed those exciting words, "Da, Da."

But now I am in the hospital room with a young woman whose esophagus and stomach are lined with blisters. Years of emotional tension and turmoil have resulted in a chronic condition. And I say to her, "When you pray to your heavenly Father, He will give you peace." Instead of becoming a reassuring symbol, it brings tears as she says, "I cannot pray. My memories of my father are so negative they get in the way of me mentally when I try to pray."

What has happened to the beautiful symbol, the bringing together of a word about the sky and the reassuring term "father"? For this young woman the symbol is blocked by the reality of a father with whom she has been in conflict for years.

The words "heavenly Father" are an enrichment of the term father and thus become a symbol. For me it brings back memories of lying on my back in the shade of an apple tree behind our house in British Columbia and seeing the fluffy clouds float by, forming and reforming into animals, flowers, and birds as they passed my line of vision. So for me, the addition of "heavenly" adds feelings of awe, majesty, unspeakable beauty to the word "father," as a symbol should. It is the sin, the dissonance in our life that blocks the transmission of the message in the symbol.

Take a few minutes to write down other symbolic statements about God. Is there one that is especially meaningful to you, that is more expressive of a high point in your spiritual pilgrimage? What about a term that creates negative dissonance?

When you think about it, you recognize that a symbol has a hard core of reality and is not merely something so nebulous you cannot do anything with it. You see, effective religious communication will always be a piece of information plus.

You may be saying to yourself, "Where does this leave the Holy Spirit? Isn't it the Holy Spirit who makes truth come alive in the heart and mind of the reader?"

Yes, that is the function of the Holy Spirit, the same Holy Spirit who inspired the writers of the Old Testament and New Testament to use symbolic language to convey God's message. Since the extremely creative God created us in His image, that is the most effective means he employs to communicate to us now. And if we do not use symbol and metaphor to communicate God's message to today's generation, we are actually subverting the way in which the Holy Spirit operates in our reader's heart and mind.

And when you study the truly life-changing sermons of the great preachers you will find they hit home better and strike deeper chords because they have been enriched by symbol and metaphor.

More than 65 years ago I was a young preacher studying at a Bible college. I had developed a pattern of preaching based on the models I had in my church and a small local Bible school. I used a lot of straightforward statements, laced with a lot of quotations from Scripture. But at Bible college I discovered the *Treasury of David* and other compilations of sermons by Charles Haddon Spurgeon. I found that once I had prepared my sermon I could gain tremendously by reading Spurgeon's sermon on that text. His use of imagery, of anecdote, stimulated me so much I was able to enrich my sermon as well.

Let's move to the area of personal evangelism. What has been the most effective evangelistic piece for many decades? The *Four Spiritual Laws*, without question. When they were first used, Bill Bright insisted that you share them one-on-one from memory, drawing the illustrations on either a napkin or a piece of paper as you shared the rather basic truth about sin and salvation. He believed the informality was the secret for the success they were experiencing.

Staff spent five years trying to convince Bill Bright to let someone print up the Four Spiritual Laws. Since then, approximately two billion have been printed and distributed, and those using the printed version have been as effective as those who doodled on napkins. In fact, a British version that does not even use the term "Spiritual Laws" but talks about knowing God personally is just as effective.

Why?

There are several reasons. One is the effective integration of verses from the Bible. Another is that at each stage the counselee is forced to make a decision, so the process actually becomes a series of decisions that result in a prayer rather than one giant leap of faith.

Yet I believe that a significant reason for the success of this little booklet is the use of symbols to express man's deepest feelings and relationships. The Holy Spirit is able to appeal to men and women not merely at the cognitive, the learning-about-facts level. He is able to appeal at a much deeper and more strongly motivational level, the way people feel about themselves and their relationships, through symbol.

What we tend to forget in our communications is that the human being is one in whom the earthly is an image of the transcendent. God graciously reveals himself in a way which respects that fact. He does not blot out our normal faculties of communication in a blinding visible manifestation of himself. Nor, on the other hand, does He use computer language to be read without imagination.

What do we read in Hebrews 1:1–47?

The Son, Jesus Christ, became a living, breathing, walking and talking symbol of the Father. He said, "I and the Father are one." Because of the limitations of the human body, Paul reminds us in Philippians 2:7 (NASB) that "He emptied himself, taking the form of a bond-servant, and being made in the likeness of men. And being found in appearance as a man, He humbled himself by becoming obedient to the point of death, even death on a cross."

Now when Zinzendorf saw the picture of the dying Christ, he saw and experienced a lot more than the death of a man on the cross. After all, people were crucified rather regularly. Even the death of a disciple like the beloved John would have been little more than the death of another man. Only as Zinzendorf, and by the same token you and I, see the dying God symbolized by Christ, who is very God of very God, does the crucified achieve redemptive significance. He literally "bore our sins in his own body on the tree" and suffered the punishment we deserved for our sin, thus forever wiping out the judgment against us for our sin.

It is because the picture of Christ as a symbol of what Christ has done for us penetrated so deeply into the innermost being of Zinzendorf that it galvanized him into action. We see so little action in our churches, I am convinced, because our communication is at the word and truth level, not the soul and spirit level possible through metaphor and symbol.

Let me illustrate from Jesus' preaching. Let's examine the story of the Lost Sheep in Luke 15:4-6. What is the truth Jesus is teaching in this story? That Jesus "came to seek and to save that which is lost." Yet what are the symbolic overtones that strike such deep emotional roots in us? The sheep as a helpless creature, the fact the Shepherd personally went after the one that had gone astray, the rejoicing over the finding of the lost sheep, the news he carried it in his arms.

Or consider Hebrews 12:1. What is the truth? Perseverance in the faith. What are the symbolic overtones of the metaphors used?

Now that we have considered the significance of the symbol and metaphor and how the Holy Spirit has used it in biblical communication, let's examine how we as writers can use imagery.

### 1. Word Pictures

*In Fearfully and Wonderfully Made* Paul Brand describes the cell structure of the body, comparing it with the body of Christ, the church. After describing some of the strange members of the church, he recognizes how God uses the diversity to achieve His goal, and Brand writes, "The chuckle at Christ's body is caught in my throat like cotton."[1]

What is the symbol? Cotton. What do we call words that follow as or like? Simile.

Write the words "righteousness of God." Now put down two or three comparisons. Now write down "unrighteous man," and pair it with a simile. Isaiah has an apt simile in chapter 57, verse 20: "The wicked are like the troubled sea when it cannot rest."

*In Celebration of Discipline* Richard Foster writes, "Prayer catapults us onto the frontier of the spiritual life."[2] What kind of imagery is that? Metaphor.

An extended metaphor is used by Wilbur Rees is in the title of one of his books: *$3 Worth of God.*

As an exercise for yourself write down metaphors for the guilt of sin.

Metaphors need not be serious at all times. They can be humorous.

## 2. Parables from Life

A little more than 60 years ago a young Southern Baptist cut a record comparing the Christian life to a football game. I was selling records in Moody Bookstore at that time and quickly became aware of its popularity. In fact, it was so popular the author launched a record company and a publishing venture. It became Word Inc., though they recently changed their name to W Publishing. The young man was Jarrell McCracken.

What does that tell us? That a parable from life has the unique ability to communicate widely and touch people deeply. Unfortunately, few communicators use the parable, possibly because it requires considerable creative powers.

Bruce Olson was a brash youngster of 19 when he tried to penetrate the Bari tribe on the border of Colombia and Venezuela for Christ. He nearly died in the process, but eventually gained the respect and ears of the Bari. And when he did, he was able to help them understand the incarnation by using one of their folk tales as a parable of what God had done in Christ.

Here is the story Bruce Olson told in one of his letters:

Adabadora finished his share in the community hunt early and was awaiting reunion with the chieftain and other warriors at the previously selected landmark. He was resting on the jungle floor, squatting in a position from which he could spring into action should the wild pigs reappear.

Looking down, he noticed many ants to the side of his foot. They reminded him of his own people, the Bari. Adabadora was convinced they were attempting to build an anthill, but it was obvious from a Bari point of view that they did not know how to do it. The form was unfunctional as well as unpleasant.

Adabadora reached down, digging his fingers through the decaying moist leaves into the light brown jungle earth. He was going to help the ants shape a hill suitable for community life. The ants though were frightened by this great and unknown "force" and scattered to hide wherever cover could be found. Again, and with even greater force, he moved the earth and began molding it into the familiar Bari oval pattern, a shape like a Bari community longhouse. Though the great force exerted by Adabadora was meant to be beneficial, his intervention had frightened the ants.

Disgusted with their fright, Adabadora decided to stamp out the ants with his heavy foot. Just then the silence was broken by a macaw parrot screeching a mating call. That was a reassurance to the ants that the "force" no longer was a danger. They reappeared from their hiding places.

Adabadora had his foot lifted high to smash the ants when a startling thing happened. The ants were all aware of a static Power that glowed in a quick flash. Then the ants realized they had a strange new community member. It was Adabadora, who had been transformed into an ant.

As an ant, Adabadora spoke ant language, ate ant food, and worked like the other ants. He worked on the community undertaking, building sand by sand that unfunctional anthill. In vain he tried to tell the ants of a better-shaped hill that would be more functional. He told them how to plan the trails from the four directions of the wind to converge on the community hill. He told them about growing delicious fungus. But none of the ants accepted what he said. No one believed his words. At one time he even told the ants he was once that "force" that had moved the earth to shape a community hill for them. But the ants only ridiculed him.

A second time that Power was felt in the ant community. Adabadora reappeared in human form, transformed back into Bari. Again he reached through the moist decomposing jungle leaves into the soil, where with rigid fingers he dug into the earth. He moved the earth into the familiar shape of a Bari longhouse. He planned the trails from the four winds by which to enter the community hill. He plotted the up and down trails, and those which even went deeper into the earth where fungus is now grown to nourish the ants.

Of course, the ants were frightened when the earth moved again. But that instant flash of Power had also communicated peace, just as the sun rays filter warmth and illumination through the leaves of the high trees into the undergrowth in which we all live. Now the ants continue to build an anthill identical to the Bari community longhouse, but only in miniature.

In the same fashion God had a precious message to communicate to the Bari. He also was not understood when He spoke through expressions in His creation. Then when

God became human in our flesh and lived among us, spoke human language, worked as a human and taught us His ways, many ridiculed. But some believed because they had seen the Power.

Bruce Olson effectively used this parable to communicate a heavenly idea in earthly terms. Is that not how Jesus did it? Read Luke 14:16–24. What is the essential truth being portrayed? How does Jesus involve our emotions as he tells the story? What could result from reading this parable?

### 3. Stories from Life

One of the facts about Jesus that Luke had to get across was that he could do all things in the power of the Father. He could simply have written to Theophilus, "My dear friend. I have done a lot of research about Jesus. Believe me, he was incredibly powerful. God himself demonstrated His power through Jesus."

Now that would have been a statement of fact, the kind I *hear* often from the pulpit and often see in print when I read sermons. It's the "I'm telling you the truth, brothers and sisters, because it is true."

Luke, however, realized that if people were not only to read about the power of Jesus but actually experience it emotionally as they read the account, he would have to tell stories about Jesus. Thus He and the other gospel writers tell stories that paint Jesus larger than life, turning him into a heroic, almost mythic character. Take Luke 9:12-17, where you have the feeding of the 5,000. This is followed by the classic exchange between Christ and His disciples that leads Peter to say, "Thou art the Christ."

Luke's next scene is the transfiguration, where three disciples see Jesus, Moses, and Elijah in supernatural bodies (Luke 9:28–36). Notice how Luke ties this event to reality, "Some eight days after these sayings. . ." And he concludes this series of stories with the experience of the demon-possessed boy whom the disciples could not heal. The powerless disciples are contrasted with the all-powerful Jesus.

And how do we use these stories of Jesus? We pull them out of their larger context to expound on a single truth. We may have the correct heavenly idea, but we fail to let the series of stories achieve their life-changing impact by isolating the story. The successful writer today does what Luke did.

Joyce Landorf's book, *Irregular People* contains one vast, expanded treatment of one heavenly idea: that all of us have a person or persons in our life with whom, for whom, we can do nothing—we have to leave that irregular person up to God. The central, extended illustration is her father.

### 4. Allegory/Comparison

The church fathers used allegory a lot. Because they overdid it, there was a reaction to this form of communicating heavenly ideas. Yet Paul effectively uses the allegory in Galatians 4:24-31. And John Bunyan's classic *Pilgrim's Progress* is now being joined by several books by writers in our day.

### 5. By Using Terms that Make God Active

Do you want to actively engage the mind and heart of your reader? Then write in an active, virile, colorful style. Do you want to portray a God involved in the world and its people? Then use language that portrays God through action words.

What do you want to communicate to the people you face in the pews on Sunday? To the reader who will buy what you write? You determine the level of communication by the imagery you use, by the kind of language you employ.

### 6. By Employing Variety of Literary Devices

Let me illustrate just some variations that will help you to more effectively communicate heavenly ideas in earthly terms.

One of the Psalms that has stuck in my memory from adolescence is Psalm 103. Let's do a quick tour of some of the literary devices employed by the Psalmist.

Repeat for emphasis (1-2)

Parallelism (3-5)

Statement and illustration (6-7)

Statement of what is not against what is (9-11)

Comparison (11-13)

Simile (15)

Metaphor (19)

If we really believe the Bible is God's communication to man, let's use the same tactics to communicate heavenly ideas in earthly terms. You'll be amazed at the increase in power in your communication because you will begin to reach your reader at all levels, not merely the mind.

# 27

## Integrating Scripture and Life Experience in Writing

There were three of us in a Holiday Inn restaurant in Victorville, California: Dan Benson, our editorial director at Here's life Publishers, Dale Evans Rogers, and I. Our goal was to see if we could get Dale to write a book for us. When we asked her what was on her heart, she said that she wanted to write a book on humility, which she said was in really short supply, especially in the Hollywood culture in which she and Roy still moved. Yet every editor or publisher she had talked to about the book had said, "No, thank you. Humility does not sell."

As we talked, an idea came to me, so I asked her: "What if we were to use the analogy of being in the Master Potter's hands? That would indicate dependency upon God, one of the indicators of humility." She perked up, and after discussing the possibility said, "I don't know anything about pottery, but if you do, let's do it."

We issued a contract and signed her up for the book. Then when Here's Life Publishers was sold to Thomas Nelson they engaged Dan as editor. A couple of months later he received agreement to engage me as writer for the Dale Evans Rogers' book.

With access to all of Dale's out of print books, I developed an outline of experiences that could fit into the analogy of being in the hands of the Master Potter. I prepared questions for each chapter and began interviewing Dale for her experiences in the context of the pottery imagery.

Yet I wanted more than just another book of Dale's experiences, and with her permission was able to add biblical passages and examples that tied into hers' and Roy's experiences. My goal was to integrate life experience and biblical truth in such a seamless way that the person reading only for Dale's experiences would also get hooked by the biblical accounts.

I believed, and still do, that when you have only experience in an article or book, you are exposing specific life experiences that, while inspirational and occasionally life-changing, are too easily misinterpreted, either by you as author or the reader. On the other hand, I have been aware of many people who knew the Bible extremely well, and in some cases had memorized a lot of it, but never experienced the intimacy of a vital, ongoing relationship with Christ and thus did not exhibit the love, grace and mercy—and commitment to truth—of our Savior.

Now let me give you an example from the Dale Evans Rogers' book *In the Hands of the Potter,* which lists me as co-author on the cover (now out of print):

> My ego manifested itself very early. When I got hurt, instead of going to the Lord and saying, "I want you to pick up the pieces, please, and put me back together again. Make me what you want me to be," I just straightened my back and said, "I will show you."[1]

How different is the attitude expressed by Isaiah:

> But now, O Lord, you are our Father; we are the clay, and you our potter; and all we are the work of Your hand. (Is. 64:8 KJB).

But isn't the idea of God's demanding control over our lives an Old Testament concept? Didn't Jesus bring us a new freedom, a new relationship with God?

Yes, He did. Yet as strange as it may seem, the idea of our being clay and God being the Master Potter shows up in New Testament writings as well. The apostle Paul made clear reference to it in his letter to the Romans:

> But, indeed, O man, who are you to reply against God? Will the thing formed say to him who formed it, "Why have you made me like this?" Does not the potter have power over the clay, from the same lump to make one vessel for honor and another for dishonor? (Rom. 9:20–21 NASB)

With that as backdrop I was able to integrate the life experiences of Dale and Roy Rogers with biblical insights for a book that made it to the top 17 in sales.

## 1. Dialoging with readers mentally and emotionally involves them

When I was given the assignment of turning a manuscript on decision-making into a more popular and more evangelical book, *Making the Right Decision* (long out of print) I depicted a Christian family in the throes of making a decision to move from California to New Hampshire, where the father had a lucrative job waiting for him. First I described the couple using the two column approach, listing positives in one and negatives in the other. The result was no clear direction. The following paragraph asks:

> What was wrong with Sherry's approach? Was it Doug's clearly depressed mood? Had they missed a clear pro or a strong negative con? What should have gone into their

attempt at decision-making? What is a decision made up of anyway?

Before we get into the answers to these questions let's see if we can pick up a few pointers from a time for decision described in the Bible. Though it took place nearly three thousand years ago, the incident had all the elements of a classic decision-making situation.

At this point I begin to describe the time when Joshua was ready to pass on the mantle of leadership and challenges Israel to make a critical decision. I quote Joshua 24:15 (NKJB):

> And if you be unwilling to serve the Lord, choose this day whom you will serve, whether the gods your fathers served in the region beyond the River, or the gods of the Amorites in whose land you dwell; but as for me and my house, we will serve the Lord.

Now I get back to the discussion of decision-making:

> The fact that the leaders of Israel had a choice that day, and that Doug and Sherry had a choice, reveals several elements in decision-making. One is that God has given all of us a mind able to determine the options. If we take the time, we can think through the elements in a situation requiring a decision, evaluating the alternatives. The

second is that each decision has automatic consequences once we act upon it. Finally, no one else can make these decisions for us and we bear the ultimate responsibility for making them, as did the leaders of Israel facing Joshua that day.

At this point as I was writing the book I could hear a reader disagree. So I engaged in a dialogue with a specific kind of reader:

> I'll go along with that, you say, but my problem is that I have difficulty making the right decision.

I rehearse Israel's three choices—and then back to the choices that Doug and Sherry faced. Then I move back to what Joshua revealed in his address to the people, that if you have a personal relationship with God, it is really much easier to make a decision. In Israel's case, they had wandered in the desert for 40 years and seen God do many marvelous things, revealing that He is indeed dependable. The decision really was not that difficult to make.

## 2. Integrating life experience and Scripture does not necessarily need the quotation of a specific Bible verse.

In their book, *Fearfully and Wonderfully Made,* Dr. Paul Brand and Philip Yancey set out to provide an extended metaphor for the church. Not surprisingly, the medical doctor chose the human body as the key analogy to carry his message.

Brand and Yancey move into a discussion of why there is deteriorating bone structure in the church, why the hard bone of doctrine has softened, ending the chapter with an example of a patient with gastritis whose mother had died of the same diagnosis, when she really had cancer—and the doctor knew it. He would not tell the hard truth.

In this example Brand and Yancey do not quote a specific Bible verse, but the paragraphs are loaded with biblical examples that bear on the truth. That's what all writers who are Christian can do, but only if they have a reservoir of biblical knowledge to draw on.

## 3. Integrating life experience and Scripture helps bring biblical truth to bear on our emotions.

In writing Jim Talley's book on *Reconcilable Differences,* I had to deal with the emotions that surfaced during and after divorce. I interviewed couples who had been divorced and were reconciled after taking Jim's course at his church in Modesto, California, and quoted them throughout the book. In discussing how friendship removes the stress of negative emotions after divorce we wrote:

Let's face it. No one really wants a divorce. Most spouses have to be pushed hard before they will take action. Judy was like that.

"Sorry, but that's not me," you may be saying. "It was good riddance of the bum, and I couldn't get rid of him fast enough for what he had done to me."

If these are your feelings, you are still stoking the fires of anger and hatred. You may just love to make him squirm when he comes to pick up the children. Yet what are the real benefits of keeping such negative emotions bubbling? How do they affect your blood pressure? What do they do to your sleep? In what ways do they affect your relationship with your children? Children are more sensitive to such feelings than you might realize.[2]

We could have stopped right there, having raised thought-provoking questions. But our book was aimed at Christians, so here's how we continued:

> The Bible has a lot to say about what all this negativity can do to you: "Cease from anger, and forsake wrath; Fret not yourself, it leads only to evildoing" (Psalm 37:8 NASB); "Do not be eager in your heart to be angry? For anger resides in the bosom of fools" (Eccl. 7:9 (NASB); and "The one who

says he is the light and yet hates his brother is in the darkness" (1 John 2:9 NASB).

A Christian filled with these emotions will not be able to develop as God intends him to develop and the Christian will not be able to live for God and His glory.

*Reconcilable Differences* remained in print for more than 25 years while making a difference. For years I kept running into people for whom the book was a lifesaver. The life experiences of the couples provided the reality that readers could identify with. Jim's experiences as counselor provided the hard-nosed reality that came from having 200 divorced people in his group at church at any one time, and Scripture provided an understanding for how God wants to act in our life, as well as the hope for life change.

## 4. Integrating life experience and Scripture can be part of the experience described

Years ago John Sherrill wrote a book on how reading Scripture passages daily from a book entitled *Daily Light* had changed his life. In chapter after chapter he told how a daily reading had impacted him. My most vivid memory is of his experience with wine. He saw no reason not to have a glass of wine with dinner. Over time it became a second glass later in the evening. Then it became a glass at lunch—and sometimes a glass just to make him feel good.

One day the Scripture passages focused on not being drunk with wine but filled with the Spirit. It was like the Lord hit him over the head. He knew he had become addicted to wine and God was speaking to him about it. He took immediate steps to correct his behavior. In that long-out-of-print book there was a remarkable integration of life experience with Scripture.

When Scripture becomes our bread of life, it feeds us with the most nourishing spiritual food we can take in and it can shape our life.

**5. Life experiences and Scripture can be integrated for a better understanding of Jesus' experience and awaken us to new sensitivities.**

Max Lucado provides us with one of the most poignant examples of this in his book, *No Wonder They Call Him the Savior*. Read it to see how he uses a life experience to deepen our understanding of the suffering of Jesus on the cross. (see p. 43, *The Cry of Loneliness*).

**6. What is necessary to achieve these goals in our writing?**

I call it biblical literacy at a level few writers achieve because they will not make the effort. My biblical knowledge grew through four years of Bible classes in a Christian high school, two years of biblical studies in a Bible institute, and two more years at a Bible college. But I also studied the Bible in preparation for the preaching I was doing and as a Sunday school teacher at every level from the preteen to the adult level.

Most readers are able to mentally distance themselves from a biblical example as something that happened "then." But by following a biblical example with a contemporary life experience, we immediately show how relevant the Bible is to our life experiences today.

## 28

# Earning the Right to Be Published

Ever since God created Adam and Eve our task as God's followers has been to express the creative calling He gave them. Yet if we create and no one knows about it, we may have a wonderful sculpture, painting, article or book, even web site, and still not be His messenger. The message encapsulated in what we have created has to get to at least one other person for us to fulfill God's calling. For writers I call that "Earning the Right to Be Published," for publishing is one of God's ways of passing on His creative message.

So what earned Jerry Jenkins and Tim LaHaye the right to be published in the Left Behind series, with more than 63 million adult and teen books sold? Consumers bought more copies of *Desecration*, the ninth book in the series in three months than any novel, secular or religious, in the first year. By the summer of 2001 more than 5,000 people had sent letters to the publisher and authors saying they had accepted Christ after reading one of the books.

And what earned Bruce Wilkinson and Dave Kopp the right to be published as *The Prayer of Jabez?* That book sold more copies the first year of publication than any non-fiction book ever in the known history of publishing—three million more copies than the nearest candidate, the book by Oprah Winfrey's cook. We're talking eight million copies in the first year.

That means in 2002 secular magazines, including *Publishers Weekly* and *New York Times*, had to swallow their pride and report that two religious books, one of them religious fiction and the other religious non-fiction, outsold every other book released by the big New York houses that year.

You don't have to consider the Left Behind series great literature—thousands of writers don't, feeling quite confident they could write better fiction. And you don't have to agree with Bruce Wilkinson's central thesis in *The Prayer of Jabez* to appreciate what God has done with that little book in shaking up the establishment, both Christian and non-Christian, in publishing.

Then another upstart began showing muscle. Released in 2002 by Zondervan, *The Purpose Driven Life* by Rick Warren galloped onto the bestseller lists. Then Rick and his people developed the 40 Days of study of *The Purpose Driven Life* and Zondervan pushed it into churches for use in developing small groups. Sales jumped to two million a month.

If you talk to Jerry Jenkins, Bruce Wilkinson, Rick Warren, or their publishers, they all say, "It's a God thing." And they are right.

Now if it's a God thing, why think about it in terms of "Earning the right to be published"? Okay, consider *The Prayer of Jabez*. For 30 years Bruce Wilkinson gave messages on that prayer. He even put it on tape and offered it for sale. Bruce took time to write a major book on the Prayer of Jabez—what the prayer meant to him was that important. Guess what? Fifteen publishers turned him down and it sat on a shelf or in a drawer for years. Somehow Multnomah got involved and assigned David Kopp to the project and he produced the 92-page version. Yes, a writer got involved, a writer who knew what the Gospel writer Luke learned in the first decades after Christ's death, as described in Luke 1:1–4 (NASB).

"Inasmuch as many have undertaken to compile an account of the things accomplished among us, just as those who from the beginning were eyewitnesses and servants of the word have handed them down to us, it seemed fitting for me as well, having investigated everything carefully from the beginning, to write it out for you in consecutive order, most excellent Theophilus; so that you might know the exact truth about the things you have been taught"(Luke 1:1–4, NASB).

What do I see in these verses that earned Luke the right to be published? Let me list the reasons first and then elaborate on them.

1. **Luke had a target reader clearly in mind . . . Theophilus.**
2. **Luke did market research to determine what was already available on the topic.**
3. **Luke did additional research to discover the true facts about Jesus' life, death and resurrection.**
4. **Luke selected and organized his materials for maximum impact on the reader.**
5. **Luke had a clear purpose for writing his book and constantly kept that in mind.**

Now let's examine these five reasons more closely.

### 1. Luke Had a Target Reader Clearly in Mind

Take a look at verse three. What is the name of the target reader?

Theophilus.

What mental images arise when you see that name? That's right, the name tells us that Theophilus was a Greek. In addition, based on the period when Luke wrote this Gospel, I think I'm safe in assuming he was a new Christian.

Now if you had been writing a book for a Greek, what kind of book would you have written? I think I might have been tempted to say, "All Greeks are philosophers, so I'll write an *Evidence that Demands a Verdict,* like Josh McDowell and his associates did, or possibly *Mere Christianity,* like C.S.Lewis did. I would have been tempted to load it with quotes from Greek philosophers that revealed the emptiness of their philosophy and the superiority of Christ's philosophy.

Yet Luke did exactly the opposite of that. He stayed clear of a tightly-reasoned philosophical treatise, instead compiling what is largely a book of stories about Jesus, interspersing it with pithy sayings by Jesus and parables told by Jesus.

Ever hear someone criticize a book by saying, "That's just a bunch of anecdotes. He may be able to tell a good story, but I really would prefer some meaty content?"

I can just imagine the book review editor of the Corinthian Times saying, "We really don't need another book of experiences. We're having enough trouble with people who think the Christian life is all experience, and here's Luke giving us all these experiences of the disciples who were with Jesus."

Yet because Luke had his reader clearly in mind, he was not a bit worried about any criticism of his book of stories. You see, they are stories about

- Jesus at work in the lives of people;
- People dominated by Satan who needed Jesus to release them;
- The way God built His kingdom.

Consider the story found in Luke 10:10-37, commonly described as the story of the Good Samaritan. What makes this story worthy of being published, remembering that Luke is writing to a new Christian who is Greek?

Here are some reasons I see as I study the story:

a. Being attacked by robbers was and is a common occurrence, providing instant reader identification.

b. It evokes a strong emotional response among readers. They get angry at the thieves who beat the man, feel strong sympathy for the beaten man, and again get angry at the religious leaders passing by on the other side. Finally, they rejoice at the Samaritan stopping to help the beaten man.

c. The story provides both a negative and a positive role model. The negative role models are the religious leaders who pass by, while the positive role model is the Samaritan.

d. The story travels well cross-culturally, giving it a universal appeal. Religious leaders of all cultures have similar attitudes--and help usually comes from the most despised in society.

e. The hero is not a Jew. In fact, he is from among the downtrodden, awakening the reader's sympathy and a desire to imitate his actions.

f. It is application-oriented, with specific action illustrated. So it is not merely a laying on of guilt.

Imagine the story stopping after the Levite had gone by. Great for someone who uses guilt as a motivator. Instead, Jesus ends the story on a positive note of hope--the beaten man is well taken care of in an inn while the Samaritan goes about his business.

Clearly, the story is a communication tool without peer. That's why Matthew, speaking of Jesus, writes, "He did not speak to them without a parable." (Matthew 13:34 NASB). Mark confirms that Jesus never spoke to those listening to him without including a parable, stories as we call them, in chapter 4, verse 34.

The story is also highly personal, since it touches each of us at our own point of need. Some of you are speakers, and I'm sure you do what I do when I address a crowd. I find the really responsive two or three and speak at them. I realized early that if you speak at the mass of people you lose all of them, but focus on two or three and you start getting results.

My goal as a writer and literary agent is to change lives through the books I write or represent. If we are going to do that, we need the same focus on one life that needs to be changed.

I remember talking to Margaret Jensen about her target reader when she began work on the manuscript for *Violets for Mr. B.* She said she wanted to reach nurses who were defeated and negative, making them laugh at some of the funny things that occur in nursing as well as gaining a new perspective on how God could use them.

In my more than 65 years in journalism I've written a weekly editorial for a denominational paper, feature articles for major publications, a children's story column, a boys' Bible study column, curriculum for inner city teens, curriculum for adults and for boys in Christian Service Brigade, plus many articles for the captains of industry.

How have I been able to target my material for such a diverse readership? For one thing, I do not think of them as readerships. I think of one person in that age group, that social strata, and zero in on that person's way of thinking and way of living. That's how I can communicate to readers as diverse as your eight-year-old son and the chairman of the board of the Mitsui Group in Japan.

Tim LaHaye had written 40 non-fiction books before he teamed up as theologian with Jerry Jenkins, the writer. One of his books had sold two million copies. Tim told us at the Writing for the Soul Conference that as he wrote he kept a reader with a sixth grade education in his mind's eye.

In 1963 I had the privilege of interviewing Dr. Helmut Thielicke of Germany on what he considered great preaching. After he described his preparation routine, he concluded with the statement, "Then I go into the marketplace to discover how to apply what I have learned."

Now let's consider your book or article idea. Who is the target reader? What does she or he look like, think about, feel? If you are to become his or her mentor through a book or article, what do you need to learn about him or her? And what must you do to keep that reader clearly in focus as you write?

The second reason Luke earned the right to be published is that

## 2. Luke Researched the Market for What Was Available

Take a quick look at verses one and two of Luke chapter one, "Inasmuch as many have undertaken to compile an account of the things accomplished among us, just as those who from the beginning were eyewitnesses and servants of the word have handed them down to us."

What did Luke do before he began to write? Yes, he thoroughly checked with what was already circulating about the life of Jesus. Now that may be a bit disconcerting to some, for Luke seems to be saying he did some rather considerable research into what was available.

It is generally conceded by Bible scholars that Mark and Matthew were already circulating by the time Luke wrote his gospel. There may also have been other reports of Jesus' activities circulating. What Luke is telling us is that he is well aware of these. If he were alive today, he undoubtedly would have checked his local Christian bookstore thoroughly before he began writing.

I've represented a Christian motivational speaker who consistently addresses the top leaders in the business world. And helping them understand the importance of a vision is part of his message. But when I tried to market his book on *Vision Quest* I drew yawns from publishers—that topic had been well-covered in both the Christian and secular market. And even though as a speaker the author could sell a lot of books, he still had to have a unique angle.

The acquisitions editor who is not aware of what the competition is doing is not true to the calling of God in his life. By the same token, the author who is content to write without market research deserves to receive a stream of rejection letters.

You see, God used Luke's background as a doctor to bring us a unique slice of Jesus' life. Who else gives us the story of Zacharias going dumb? Of Mary going to Elizabeth and magnifying the Lord with that marvelous Magnificat? Of the shepherds on the hills of Bethlehem visited by angels.

Can you imagine Matthew, that Jewish specialist who repeatedly quotes from the Psalms of David, passing up the shepherd's story?

Where but in Luke do you find the troubling, yet heartwarming story of a 12-year-old Jesus left behind by his parents, only to find him confounding the wise men of Israel?

Who includes the three parables about prayer that Jesus told? See Luke 11:5–13; 18:2–5; 18:10–14. And I find it instructive to compare the story of the healing of the Centurion's servant in Luke 7:1–10 with that in Matthew 8:5–13. Or look at the extra detail Luke provides compared to Mark when he tells the story of the two disciples on the road to Emmaus (Luke 24:13–35 vs. Mark 16:12–13).

We go to Luke to find Christ's heartbeat for the poor, to gain insights into medical conditions in Jesus' day, to understand how vital a part women played during Jesus' ministry on earth. You cannot exclude women from serving Jesus in a wide variety of ways if you read Luke carefully and prayerfully.

In 1980 I looked at what was available on the market and realized there was not a single book focusing on inductive Bible study for preteens, so I packaged a collection of Dash Magazine Bible study articles I had written and sold them as *Preteen Bible Exploration*. When the Billy Graham people saw the book they were intrigued, for they did not have a Bible study book for follow-up with children. For years children around North America received copies of my book once they had completed the initial follow-up materials. It happened because I saw a need in the market.

In 1986 we received a manuscript that had been rejected by Word Books because the author was unknown. We knew Jan Frank was a speaker for CLASS, an organization that promotes Christian women speakers nationwide. We also realized *A Door of Hope,* a book about being sexually molested by her father, and the ten steps she and others had to take to deal with the pain even as adults, was truly unique. There was no other book on incest written by a victim who was also a licensed family counselor and a speaker. She had found a niche market. Twenty-four years later that book was still in print.

## 3. Luke Did His Own Research on the Life of Christ

Luke makes this clear in verse three, when he writes, "It seemed fitting for me as well, having investigated everything carefully from the beginning, to write it out for you in consecutive order, most excellent Theophilus." (NASB)

Now the only time period when Luke was in Palestine long enough to do this kind of research appears to be the two years that Paul was in prison in Caesarea. Can you, in your imagination, see Dr. Luke trudging the Roman roads in Palestine, tracking down witnesses to events in Jesus' life? I'm sure the apostle Paul must have been on his mind a lot, but he kept at his research. If you've ever wondered what good came out of Paul's imprisonment in Caesarea, the Gospel According to Luke is probably a major one.

Research is, unfortunately, not a strong point with most Christian writers. Those who do research really stand out. I think of Dr. Warren Wiersbe, who for years read a sermon each day in addition to his other research. And when I read the books of Charles Swindoll I see that a lot of research has gone into his material.

James Michener has been one of the most popular American writers. He spent years of meticulous research for every novel he wrote. He lived in the area he was going to write about for long periods, digging into the history of the region in great depth, and took the time to visually absorb the environment. No wonder he could write 900-page books that sell better than most short books.

Holly Miller, at the time editor of the Saturday Evening Post, told me in an interview that most Christian writers do not interview enough people in researching for an article. She recommends five to six interviews for every article. In her case her article series on women today was quickly recognized by a book editor as unique and she received a book contract for articles she had written.

When I examine the Gospel According to Luke, I sense that he has interviewed scores of people, mulled over the implications of Jesus' life and the vitriolic opposition of the Jewish religious leaders. Thus his research resulted in more than a merely mechanical retelling of events. Rather, through the energizing of the Holy Spirit, his material became the creative and dramatic overview of the greatest life ever lived.

The kind of knowledge required to write significant Christian literature is felt knowledge, a blend of passion and clear-sighted awareness of reality. When your research results in that kind of knowledge, then you are not merely a technician, fitting words together to gain X number of dollars in royalty. Nor is it only the expression of a dilletante who likes to play with words and see how they fit together.

Research will not only vastly enrich content, it will often help shape content. Outlines may have to be scrapped in the light of new information uncovered by research. The interaction with the big ideas of the ages will be clearly evident as the book or article takes shape.

Research can get us the information and stories we need to write an article or a book, but we need to take a fourth step. And that relates to organizing the material for maximum impact on the reader.

### 4. Luke Organized His Material for Maximum Impact

Here's how Luke describes his approach: "to write it out for you in consecutive order . . . " (v. 3).

Have you ever examined the Gospels from the perspective of organization? Ah, you say, I do not see any special attempt at anything but a chronological sequence of events. Then why did the apostle John write, "Many other signs therefore Jesus also performed in the presence of the disciples, which are not written in this book; but these have been written that you may believe that Jesus is the Christ, the Son of God; and that believing you may have life in His name"(John 20:31)?

We may have been so busy relating this passage to John's central message, that we missed the statement about his organizational intent. So consider, for example, how the gospel writers started their books.

How does Matthew start chapter one? Right, with a genealogy. How boring, you may be saying. I can imagine Matthew submitting the manuscript to editor Horatius at Aquilla and Priscilla Publishing in Ephesus. Like most editors he looked at the first page, sighed, and said, "Another addition to the reject pile."

If it had not been for the Jewish press, it probably would never have been published. Yet Matthew knew that the Jewish reader of his day was fascinated by genealogies, so he hooked his reader with the genealogy of Jesus.

Let's turn to Mark, probably greatly influenced in his approach to writing by that activist, the apostle Peter. No genealogy for him. He just loved the story of that preacher of fire and brimstone, John the Baptist. He could really make the crowd cringe, even the Roman soldiers. So for all other activists he started with John the Baptist in the desert, people flocking to him from all over. Mark loves crowds, as did Peter, and he has "all the people of Jerusalem" turning out for this itinerant preacher.

Now let's go to Luke. Here's the medical man, deeply concerned over a barren woman, a future father struck dumb, and the miracle of birth by a virgin. Luke saw the significance of the story of Zacharias, of the appearance of the angel to the virgin, Mary, and the miracle that both births represented. For Theophilus, the Greek, the supernatural was as much a part of his life as philosophy. The supernatural surrounding the birth of Christ and his forerunner, John the Baptist, was *The Evidence that Demands a Verdict* in terms of life commitment.

Even today the Christian writer's task is to give us a precise slice of life that has unity and coherence. It must have internal and external consistency and validity. Only through a unity inherent in the plan and in the selection of materials chosen can any written material give us the fullest satisfaction.

Have you ever heard someone say about an article or a book, "There's something missing" or "It doesn't quite hang together?" That happens when the Christian writer has not established the kind of unity that we see in God-- and feel in us as persons in His image. For when people say that literature must communicate truth, they mean, among other things, that it must convey unity—all the parts must fit together for a perfect whole.

Yet the selection process is to do more than that. It is also designed to give us the slice of life from the proper perspective as a Christian. Failure to do this leads us to all kinds of tangents. We become too experience-oriented, or we fail to recognize the role of experience. We see God as a great judge, and do not experience His love—or vice versa.

In presenting this balanced approach to the Christian life we must remember that Jesus and the writers of the epistles do not present truth in isolation from life. They did not present truth for truth's sake—only as it applied in life situations as a corrective, as a motivator to holiness, as the instigator of hope. Thus some of the greatest teaching in the Bible is in response to a specific life situation, described in sometimes embarrassing detail.

I am convinced that as communicators we must go beyond information to imagination, motivation and action suggestions if we want to change lives. Thus we must keep all four elements in mind when organizing our material— just as Luke did.

I have come to see the article or book as a movement. The reader is to be moved from Point A on a continuum to Point B in terms of information, motivation, and action, with imaginative presentation of truth as the key to presenting transcendent truth in humanly perceivable forms. And every article or book needs to keep all four elements in mind as the material is outlined and developed.

Finally, I notice that

## 5. Luke Had a Clear Purpose

As Luke settled into his chair to pick up the quill, he had a distinct purpose in mind for his book manuscript. Let me read it for you: "So that you might know the exact truth about the things you have been taught" (Luke 1:4 NASB).

Luke wanted to provide written assurance for Theophilus for all he had been taught verbally. The material was to recreate again and again the scenes of Jesus' miraculous ministry, His atoning death, and His validating resurrection.

If you have a clear purpose for writing your article or book it will infuse everything you put on paper, or into the computer, with a central dynamic that both guides you as a writer and aids in the communication to the reader. If this purpose grows out of your commitment to helping fulfill God's purpose on this earth, it will carry you through the many moments when you are discouraged. Finally, your book or article will have the desired result in the life of the reader.

One of the most significant books I have been associated with was *Daktar/Diplomat of Bangladesh,* by Dr. Viggo Olson. From the beginning his purpose was not to satisfy Christian curiosity, or to raise money for the Malumghat Christian Memorial Hospital in Bangladesh, but to bring fellow medical professionals to faith in Christ. He perceived his conversion from agnosticism to faith, and the many hair-raising experiences in Bangladesh, as the hook to get the reader into and through the book. His commitment to Jesus Christ, the many answers to prayer, the response of those in Bangladesh, were to be used to win over even the truly skeptical. Even the back cover material was tailored to not offend the non-believer but to hook his or her interest.

What was the result? Scores of medical people received Christ, many students in medical schools were challenged to enter medical mission work. An atheistic surgeon in Ann Arbor, Michigan, for example, was given a copy of the book just before he went into the hospital for surgery. While recuperating, he read *Daktar/Diplomat in Bangladesh* and accepted Jesus Christ as Savior.

More and more this purpose must be relevant to the genuinely felt needs of the reader. Today's generation is asking, "Is it real? Is it relevant?"

Several years ago, for example, I was concerned about the jealousy I was seeing between different areas in our company—and different ministries in our church. Using the language of gang warfare, I called them turf battles. I sat down and wrote an article called "Tire Tracks on My Turf." I sent it to a denominational magazine, which published it. Then a magazine devoted to business development in under-developed countries reprinted it. The editor of Campus Crusade's newsletter for international staff was so impressed with it, he reprinted it, giving it further international outreach. Finally, another denominational publication picked it up as well. By God's grace I had touched a hot button that made it relevant internationally.

Let me go back to a book I mentioned earlier to illustrate the significance of purpose. Jan Frank had been sexually molested by her father, a Bible class teacher in an evangelical church. When she married, the memory of what her father had done kept surfacing when she tried to relate to her husband. One day she realized she was even repelled by the aftershave he used because it was the same her father had once used. She sought help from Philippian Ministries, a prayer ministry for those suffering emotionally from memories of abuse. Once she got help, she joined the prayer ministry, counseling and praying with other women who had experienced incest.

Jan Frank decided to write a book that would not only incorporate her experience of finding help, but also provide a ten-step approach to inner healing from memories of abuse. We heard about it and examined it, letting a Campus Crusade for Christ counselor read it. He was so impressed he asked for copies of the manuscript immediately so he could begin support groups using the material.

We released *A Door of Hope* in 1987, and it was an immediate success. What made it a top seller? Jan Frank had a clearly defined purpose, that of helping women who needed to be freed from the chains of emotional bondage so they could more intimately relate to their husbands and serve the Lord with gladness.

What is your purpose for writing? Unless you can write it out in one sentence and keep it before you as a lighthouse beacon while writing, you may well end up on the shoals of insignificance, or inconsequentiality.

What earns you the right to be published? Five key elements, none less significant than the other: a clearly targeted reader, knowledge of what is on the market, thoroughly researched content, organization for life change, and a clear purpose. Nothing less will do.

# 29

## Organizing Your Book for Life-Changing Impact

What is the most important role you have as a Christian book author?

- Is it to write a dramatic story of your life?
- Is it to lobby for a cause that you now represent?
- Is it to leave a legacy for your family for a family member to find in the attic two generations later?
- Maybe it's to write what you believe God has laid on your heart?

What if I told you that you can achieve all those objectives if your focus from the get-go is to achieve life change, whether in your family, in your church, in your community, in society at large?

You may suggest that's too tall an order for you. You'll let the pastors or professors, you know, the specialists, take care of that—you just want to write for the joy of producing a book that gets five stars on Amazon.

Years ago I reached the conclusion that as a Christian communicator my role was to go for life change so that as Christians, as members of today's society, we could participate in creating impetus for Holy Spirit inspired change. After all, as believers we have the Holy Spirit living in us as Christ's representative, so we have access to the power of God at truly incredible levels.

I believe the Bible provides adequate illustrations of communicating for life change. So let's go on a journey of discovery that will reveal how to write for life impact.

A good starting point is how Jesus did it. In Mark 4:34 we read, "In fact, he taught only by illustrations in his public preaching." Matthew is even more explicit in chapter 13, verse 34, "Jesus constantly used these illustrations when speaking to the crowds. In fact, because the prophets said that he would use so many, he never spoke to them without at least one illustration." (The Living Bible)

The other New Testament communicators, like Jesus, consistently presented God's message to man through stories, parables, allegories, comparisons, contrast, metaphors and similes. We as communicators need to take this admonition to heart.

## 1. The Truly Biblical Communicator Uses Symbols and Imagery

The fact is that the Bible is the greatest repository of symbols and imagery available to us. We also must use symbols and imagery if we want to communicate God's ideas, and our knowledge about God. At this point let's look at only one example, Psalm 91:1–9, where the writer focuses on God as our refuge in the storms of life. He uses a whole series of word pictures that graphically portray the various dangers we face--and how God delivers us from all of them.

Yet beyond the fact that those who wrote the Bible, and even Christ himself, wrote and spoke with vivid word pictures, with metaphors, similes, comparisons, with symbolic statements, is there a sound psychological principle, a communications principle, underlying this approach? The fact is that we fall so far short of describing our transcendent God in ordinary words that we are really dissatisfied. Words about God simply do not do our great God justice. We must use the metaphor, the symbol to even begin to describe God in all his majesty.

As a magazine editor and freelance writer, I began to specialize in the biographical article based on a personal interview with the person. And as I accumulated these life experiences of people, I began to incorporate them into my preaching. As I went out to fill pulpits of small churches in the Chicago area and out in the communities south and west of Chicago, I discovered people especially appreciated these stories. In fact, I discovered they were starved for the reality and imagery in stories of people, who actually lived the Gospel.

In 1982, I was preparing for a writers' conference to be attended by key staff of Campus Crusade for Christ. I purchased the 10 books on the bestseller list and analyzed them for communication style. I discovered that the writers who dominated the bestseller list, some of whom still do, told stories, used parables, comparisons, symbols and metaphors to communicate what it really means to live the Christian lifestyle. Not surprisingly, I began a detailed analysis of why *Improving Your Serve*, by Charles Swindoll, should be the national bestseller. As a result, I made it exhibit No. 1 for my presentation at that staff writers' conference, and in succeeding years as I have led workshops on "Organizing Your Book for Life-Changing Impact."

What sets Swindoll's writing apart from the usual first chapter opening? He burns images into our mind that we can never escape, and they so intrigue us that we have to continue reading. But they also stimulate our imagination and change forever how we think about being a servant.

A second principle I have discovered about communicating biblically is that

## 2. The Story Is God's Preferred Style of Life-Changing Communication

When a lawyer asked Jesus, "Who is my neighbor?" Jesus did not give him a quick description or a lecture. That's probably what you and I would have done. Instead, Jesus launched into the story of the Good Samaritan (Luke 10:25). And after He told the story Jesus asked, "And which of these three do you think proved to be a neighbor to the man who fell into the robber's hands?" And the lawyer provided his own application to his life, "The one who showed mercy to him."

I compare a story like that to a time bomb. The emotional content in the story causes it to stick in the mind and heart of the listener, exploding when a life experience matches the truth in the story. Then it goes off with a powerful blast, with the truth that applies to that life situation available for application by the Holy Spirit.

A story touches us not only at the level of understanding—it awakens God-given and Holy Spirit-sharpened sensitivities to the needs of others, motivates us to do something about it, and leaves such a powerful imprint on our mind and emotions that we cannot escape our responsibility. For example, just like the story of the Good Samaritan awakens us to a whole spectrum of lifestyle truth, so it also builds emotional accountability to it in the very soul of our being. We can never walk by a suffering person without feeling a tug, without knowing we ought to help. And when we start to help we can never get by with just bandaging the wounds because the Samaritan's role model will not let us stop with that. His example holds us accountable to finish the job of helping the helpless and beaten person.

Evangelical writers have often treated Paul's letters as if they were theological treatises, which they certainly are not. Paul is operating out of his storied world. He is theologizing and ethicizing into particular situations. His letters are not an abstract collection of eternal principles that we can then link. He's a pastor preaching, if you will, proclaiming, persuading his audiences on particular points.

The question is: What was he theologizing out of? "I resolved to know nothing while I was with you," he writes to the Corinthians, "except Jesus Christ and him crucified." These are not abstract ideas. He's talking about historical events and their theological and ethical significance. So the root of the matter is the story.

When Paul thinks about sin and the fall, he thinks about Adam. When he thinks about the law, he thinks about the story of Moses. When he thinks about faith, he thinks about the story of Abraham. And, obviously, when he thinks about salvation, he thinks about the story of Jesus. So these big-ticket theological ideas are grounded in stories.

The Bible was not written in a text-oriented culture but for an oral culture. So these documents were meant to be heard. When you read them out loud in Greek, you notice alliteration and poetry and all kinds of things going on that are totally lost in translation. I think the oral dimension of the biblical world, very much connected to storytelling, is a crucial dimension and is a key to understanding the theology in those texts.

So how do we actually implement the biblical style of communication modeled by David, the prophets, Jesus and the apostles in spoken and written form? I suggest you first read Scripture with an intense focus on communication style. It will be a truly extraordinary experience; I can assure you. But then also

### 3. We Need to Study Contemporary Models Incorporating a Biblical Style of Communication

In order for you to more fully understand how biblical communication effects life change, I need to set the stage with a discussion of what I call a four-track system of communication. These four tracks strengthen the impact that results in life change.

From my perspective, all purposeful communication is a process, a movement, if you will. It is designed to move the listener or reader from Point A to Point Z through total involvement of mind, heart and all of his or her senses. Here's how we can visualize it.

A___>___>___>___>___>___>___>___>___>___Z

From where I sit, I see this process moving forward on four tracks, or levels.

**a. Information** is the basic building block of the mind. Ideas not only excite us, but they help us to make sense out of what is going on. We live by information every day, even if you walk you are guided to where you are going by information. But to effect life change, where you not only change direction on a street physically, but also change lifestyle, such information must include the knowledge of what God has said or does, for the Word of God is quick and sharper than any two-edged sword. As a journalist I have heard numerous stories illustrating how God met people simply through reading the Bible.

**b. Imagination** is undoubtedly our most effective tool in communicating transcendent ideas into humanly receivable form. I am convinced that our finite minds can simply not receive the rich fullness of God's ideas without the help of symbol and metaphor.

**c. Motivation** is God's way to move the heart, not merely titillate the intellect. But because we rarely analyze what motivates us, let me provide four key ways in which we can motivate people.

**d. Benefits** are the stock in trade of the advertising industry. Look at the ads, examine the direct mail pieces you receive. The benefits are everywhere. So if you want to motivate the reader, be sure to include personal benefits. Let me give you a biblical example where the benefits are emphasized—2 Peter 1:4, 10–11.

e. **Role Models** are a second motivator. Some years ago we had Mike McCoy, a former professional football player, in our home to share about his anti-drug ministry in high schools. He and his associates in Sports Ministries found the anti-drug emphasis a remarkable way to share their faith in Christ with higher schoolers. But why use Mike McCoy, a former professional football player? Because teens look up to professional athletes as role models.

**Emotion-involving** content is another motivator. Show business people know you need to make your audience laugh and cry. Several years ago John Stott wrote in an article in Christianity Today that we in the West need more emotional content in our Christian communication. Just think of how the story of the Prodigal Son affects your emotions . . . and motivates you to action as a result.

Josh McDowell uses emotionally powerful stories constantly as he speaks. During his speaking tours in behalf of "Why Wait?" he often told the story of receiving a phone call after a meeting one night and a young woman told him, "I've gone to bed with five men during the last five nights. Is that all there is?"

**How to** is a powerful motivational tool. Benefits get the reader's interest, role models portray the values you are trying to teach in an inspiring manner, emotional content grabs the heart, but you also need how to content to release the reader for action. Motivation alone only produces guilt--how to content releases the guilt so the reader can begin moral and productive behavior.

**Action Application** is the fourth track on which to move a reader into total involvement. One of our attempts at Here's Life Publishers to differentiate ourselves from other publishers was to have an action focus at the end of chapters. In *Building Your Mate's Self-Esteem,* by Dennis and Barbara Rainey, for example, we had the authors include an "Esteem Builder Project" at the end of chapters. These were designed to give the reader an opportunity to work through what he or she had learned in a particular way.

If you are on a writing project, what is your goal, the purpose for writing that piece?

### 4. How Do We Start?

To find out what authors of published books have done to grab the reader you might do what I just did. I pulled book after book off my shelf to see what the authors had done to grab my attention and hold it.

An autobiography of a well-known athlete follows the Contents page with a "Chronology of Events." Next comes a Foreword by a well-known pastor—useful if you are not well-enough known to be accepted as able to make a significant contribution to the reader's life. Then come two full pages of Acknowledgments, and a Prologue. On page 21 we finally start getting the experiences of the athlete. Can you see the browser paging and paging as he tries to find out if he will like the book enough to buy it? Would you, especially if you were not a sports fan, have kept going through the introductory pages?

My next book off the shelf is a book on the interior life by a well-known writer. Uh oh, same pastor wrote the Foreword as for the previous book, then a five-page Preface by the author, well-written, I might add. But it is directed at one segment of his readers—and I do not happen to fit into that segment. We've made some progress page-wise—we only need to get to page 13 for the start of the first chapter.

My next book is on marriage, though not by a counselor or psychologist. The writer is a rather well-known, highly creative person. No Foreword, Preface, or Introduction—immediately after the Contents page we are at the first chapter. And what a first chapter it is!

Treat Readers as Fellow Seekers

While the Reformation brought in a new era where everyone could read the Bible for himself or herself, only the Anabaptists camped on the implications of the priesthood of all believers. They declared themselves a brotherhood of believers, rather than establishing a hierarchy of believers who became the official proclaimers of the Word.

One of the first to treat readers, including women readers, with real dignity as intelligent believers led by the Holy Spirit, is Charles Swindoll. Just the title of the first chapter *Improving Your Serve* revealed a new attitude: "Who, Me a Servant? You Gotta Be Kidding!" The first two sentences established that he identified at eye level with the reader. On the next page he identifies further with the reader, "Perhaps that's your initial reaction, too. If so, I understand. But you're in for a pleasant surprise."[1] Similar interaction with the reader is sprinkled throughout the book.

## 5. Uses Story to Capture the Reader

So what is another approach that catches the reader off guard? Story. That's right, truth as presented in story. We can again take a cue from the apostle Paul as he writes to the Romans:

> "Against all hope, Abraham in hope believed and so became the father of many nations, just as it had been said to him, "So shall your offspring be." Without weakening in his faith, he faced the fact that his body was as good as dead—since he was about a hundred years old—and that Sarah's womb

> was also dead. Yet he did not waver through unbelief regarding the promise of God, but was strengthened in his faith and gave glory to God, being fully persuaded that God had power to do what he had promised" (Romans 4:18–21 NIV).

Stories as metaphor are another approach that catches the reader off guard. How was Gordon MacDonald, at the time senior pastor of Grace Chapel, a rapidly growing church in Lexington, Massachusetts, going to grab the attention of thoughtful, intelligent leaders in both the church and business community with a book on the interior life? Many of the classics on this topic were reflective, meditative. MacDonald decided to take the storytelling approach of Jesus as he began Chapter 2 of *Ordering Your Private World*. Entitling the chapter "The Sinkhole Syndrome," he wrote a paragraph explaining why sinkholes occur, MacDonald gets to the point he is making in the book:

> There are too many people whose lives are like one of Florida's sinkholes.[2]

Stories that are metaphors add a visual dimension to truth-telling that enhances the message by not only adding interesting information but also memory hooks. A big sinkhole is not easy to forget, nor is the truth it represents.

## 6. What Do You Want to Achieve with the First Chapter?

One of my favorite authors and family life speakers is Craig Massey, for many years a pastor. Craig was legally blind for years, so his wife read to him. They loaded up on books every trip they took, trying to keep up to date in both secular and religious literature. One day when we discussed books Craig told me, "Most books have one good idea. Normally it is presented in the first chapter, and the rest of the book is an elaboration. So we read a lot of first chapters."

Craig's comment reveals a major weakness among writers. They wade in with their big idea in the first chapter, and then try to figure out how to stretch it for a $14.95 book. In effect, they "dump the whole load" and then try to spread it for half a mile.

Yet that is not the purpose of the first chapter, in my estimation. Let me draw an analogy from speaking. When you get in front of a crowd, what do you do first? If you are an American speaker, you warm up the audience with a couple of jokes, no matter how bad they are.

The first chapter of a book similarly ought to warm up the reader to the topic and you as the writer. The readers need to feel they are going to be drawn into your circle of friendship for an intimate period of sharing.

Yet the first chapter needs to do more than warm up the reader to the topic and the author. Like an army corps of engineers, you need to build a bridge to the reader's felt need and anchor it deep in the reader's consciousness.

Across this bridge to felt need you begin to move the "freight" that will meet the reader's real need. Then what you will share will be more than a transmission of information. It will result in the stimulation of the reader's deepest heart desires.

Done well, this bridge-building establishes your credibility as the author. In most cases the reader will not have met you and thus may be a bit wary. Your identification with his or her need will give you tremendous credibility with the reader.

Furthermore, so as not to scare off the reader, or promise too much, the opening chapter should also establish the parameters of the ensuing discussion. The reader will gain a sense of what he needs to be ready for mentally if he knows what you will be discussing in the book.

To really hook the reader, you will also need to build in some of the benefits to be gained from reading your book. This gives the reader the feeling that his or her time will be profitably spent. So as you write the first chapter, remember that your reader will quickly sense whether you are dumping information or dialoging, providing authoritarian answers or embarking on a journey of discovery with the reader. The level of vocabulary, the number of anecdotes, the frequency of allusions to real life, the use of word pictures, all give the reader a feel for the kind of communication he or she will be receiving.

Let's recapitulate the goal for the first chapter:

* Warm the reader up to the topic.

* Build a bridge of felt need to the reader's real need.

* Establish the parameters of the discussion.

* Point forward to the benefits to be gained by reading the whole book.

Many writers plunge in with the actual anecdote. True, the reader will find the anecdote interesting, but sending the key idea up front prepares the reader for maximum enjoyment and learning. The reader does not have to wonder what he or she is getting into.

### 7. A Go-Get-'Em Conclusion

What has gone on behind the scenes when you see a football, basketball or soccer coach pat his player on his lower back as he sends him onto the field? The pat on the behind is but the last of a long list of motivators. In the same way, the author's conclusion is a pat on the back as he sends the reader into action. It still contains key motivational content, but no big buildup is needed. The reader has been saying "yes" so many times it is easy to say yes again.

# NOTES

Chapter 26: Communicating Heavenly Ideas

1. Brand, Paul, with Yancey, Philip: *Fearfully and Wonderfully Made*; Zondervan, Copyright 1980 by Paul Brand and Philip Yancey.

2. Foster, Richard: *Celebration of Discipline*; Harper and Row, Copyright 1978 by Richard Foster

Chapter 27: Integrating Scripture and Life Experience in Your Writing

1. Rogers, Dale Evans, with Les Stobbe: *In the Hands of the Potter*; Copyright 1994 by Dale Evans Rogers.

2. Talley, Jim: *Reconcilable Differences*; Thomas Nelson Publishers, Copyright 1985, by Jim Talley.

Chapter 29: Organizing Your Book for Maximum Life Impact

1. Swindoll, Charles R: *Improving Your Serve*; Word Books, Copyright 1981 by Word Books

2. MacDonald: *Ordering Your Private World*; Thomas Nelson Publishers; Copyright 1984 by Gordon MacDonald.

Made in the USA
Coppell, TX
03 November 2021

65154822R00140